Thank you Terry
for all the support
over so long
Lots of love
Marie

THE DUBLIN/MURPHY REPORT

Edited by John Littleton and Eamon Maher

The Dublin / Murphy Report:
A Watershed for Irish Catholicism?

the columba press

First published in 2010 by
the columba press
55A Spruce Avenue, Stillorgan Industrial Park,
Blackrock, Co Dublin

Cover by Bill Bolger
Origination by The Columba Press
Printed in Ireland by ColourBooks Ltd, Dublin

ISBN 978 1 85607 697-5

Contents

Introduction   7

1 Timothy Radcliffe OP, *Come to Me all You Who Labour*   17
2 Andrew Madden, *A Church Disgraced*   29
3 Colum Kenny, *Sacred Heart, Sacred Mind: The Challenge of Conviction in the Catholic Church*   37
4 Richard Clarke, *Parent AND Bishop*   48
5 Marie Collins, *Journey to Loss: Living the Murphy Report*   55
6 Patrick McCafferty, *Jesus The Risen Victim: A Response to the Murphy Report*   63
7 Sean O'Conaill, *The Disgracing of Catholic Monarchism*   74
8 Breda O'Brien, *Communicating the Good News and the Bad* 82
9 Eugene O'Brien, *'The boat had moved': The Catholic Church, Conflations and the Need for Critique*   90
10 Seán Ruth, *Responding to Abuse: Culture, Leadership and Change*   102
11 Enda McDonagh, *The Murphy and Ryan Reports: Between Evangelising and Priesthood*   113
12 Eamonn Conway, *Broken Hearts and not Just Torn Garments – Beginning the Discussion about Forgiveness and Healing*   121
13 Eddie Shaw, *A Personal View of a Communications Failure in a Time of Crisis*   132
14 Donald Cozzens, *Culture that Corrodes*   144
15 Garry O'Sullivan, *Quo Vadis? The Road to Rome*   148
16 Louise Fuller, *Disturbing the Faithful: Aspects of Catholic Culture under Review*   158

Editors and Contributors   171

Introduction

The past couple of decades have been momentous in terms of the diminished standing of the Catholic Church in Ireland. To gauge how far we have travelled down the road of skepticism, one has only to think back to the Papal visit in 1979, which saw massive crowds assemble at venues such as the Phoenix Park, Drogheda, Galway and Limerick. While allegedly providing a concrete sign of the good health of Irish Catholicism, in essence this visit marked the end of an era. The Church was in something of a free fall at the end of the 1970s. For some time vocations had been in decline and the deference displayed to men and women of the cloth was beginning to dissipate. A better educated laity was no longer afraid to question some of the Church's teachings on issues such as contraception, abortion and homosexuality, three areas of contention that have continued to alienate an increasing number of the laity. The Church leaders realised that trouble was brewing, which prompted an invitation to the charismatic John Paul II to come and reignite the religious fervour of the Irish people.

Fast forward to 1992 and the revelation that one of the most charismatic figures in the Irish Church, Bishop Eamonn Casey, had fathered a child with an American divorcee, Annie Murphy. He and another well-known figure, Fr Michael Cleary, had been chosen to warm up the crowd at the Papal Mass for young people in Galway in 1979. In 1993, it was also revealed that Cleary had been having a sexual relationship with his housekeeper, Phyllis Hamilton, for many years from which a son, Ross, was born. These two men had enjoyed a high media profile during the previous decade and both had been very orthodox in their pronouncements on moral issues. When the gap emerged between their public pronouncements and their personal behaviour, many commentators justifiably accused them of hypocrisy. But, while dramatic at the time, the Casey and Cleary scandals were mere trifles compared to what was in store for the Church in the following years.

In 1994 the arrest of the paedophile, Fr Brendan Smyth, whose widespread abuse of children had been highlighted by the UTV *Counterpoint* programme, added more fuel to the fire. The Pandora's box had been opened and there followed further revelations, most notably in relation to the Diocese of Ferns, where many young lives were ruined by the crimes of several paedophiles, the most notorious being Fr Sean Fortune. Colm O'Gorman made a report to the Gardaí on 9 February 1995 about the abuse he had suffered from Fortune. He did not receive much co-operation from the Church authorities in his attempts to bring Fortune to trial. Once more, it took a BBC television documentary, *Suing the Pope*, to highlight the reluctance of the institutional Church to accept the wrong perpetrated by some priests in the Diocese of Ferns. O'Gorman notes:

> The problem wasn't simply that no one told about the abuse, but that no one in the Church was prepared to act. No one in authority did anything even when they did know.
> It's not enough to speak out. Others have to be prepared to listen and to acknowledge what they have heard. They have to believe it, no matter how threatening or troubling the facts might be. And, most importantly, they have to be prepared to act.[1]

The hierarchy's failure to act has been a common feature in each of the three inquiries which have highlighted the abuse of children and the findings have been published in the Ferns (2005), Ryan (2009) and Murphy (2009) Reports. Another consistent pattern has been for Church authorities to close ranks in an attempt to limit the damage done to the institution. Denial of guilt, refusal to co-operate with the civil authorities, the victims and their families, abdication of responsibility, failure to recognise the seriousness of the problem, fear of the costs involved in any settlement, arrogant disregard for the truth through the use of 'mental reservation', are just a few of the hall-

---

1. Colm O'Gorman, *Beyond Belief* (London: Hodder and Stoughton, 2009), pp 224-5.

marks that characterise the Church's management or mismanagement of the abuse scandals.

This book is an attempt to assess the implications of the most
recent body-blow to the Catholic Church in Ireland, the Murphy
Report, published in November 2009.[2] Once more, the Murphy
Commission had its origins in a television documentary, this
time the RTÉ *Prime Time* programme *Cardinal Secrets*, produced
by Mary Raftery, with Mick Peelo as reporter. The programme
investigated the response to clerical child sex abuse allegations
in the Catholic Archdiocese of Dublin. Michael McDowell, who
was Minister for Justice at the time, set up a commission of inquiry in 2006. Its brief was to investigate how the Church and
State authorities dealt with allegations of clerical child abuse in
the period 1975-2004. Writing the day after the Report was published, Paul Cullen did not spare either the Church or the State:

> Child sexual abuse was covered up by the Dublin archdioc-
> ese and other church authorities for almost 30 years, accord-
> ing to the report of the commission of investigation.
> State authorities facilitated this cover-up by not fulfilling
> their responsibilities to ensure that the law was applied
> equally to all, and by allowing church authorities to be be-
> yond the law ...[3]

Cullen quoted the following observation from the Report:
'There was little or no concern for the welfare of the abused
child or for the welfare of other children who might come into
contact with the priest. Complainants were often met with denial, arrogance and cover-up and with incomprehension in
some areas. Suspicions were rarely acted on' [1.35]. Other revealing findings state how the Archdiocese had an 'obsessive
concern with secrecy and the avoidance of scandal' and had 'little
or no concern for the welfare of the abused child' [1.32]. Little
wonder, then, that the public reaction was one of horror and
anger. That the anger was more directed at the Church than at
the State can be explained by the fact that people rightly or

2. It should be noted that the Dublin/Murphy Report has not to date
(March 2010) been published in its entirety.
3. Paul Cullen, '30 Years of Church and State cover-up of child sex
abuse', in *The Irish Times*, 27 November 2009, p 9.

wrongly expect higher standards from priests and religious than
they do from politicians or members of An Garda Síochána. John
Waters, someone who could not be accused of pursuing a witch
hunt against the Catholic Church, drew the seemingly unavoid-
able conclusion that Murphy represents a watershed:

> The events outlined in the Murphy report have finally placed
> in doubt the Church's claim that it was ever in the business of
> implementing the Word of Jesus Christ. If this entitlement is
> to be recovered, it must be earned in shame and grief. [...]
> The sins of the Church – against children and parents, against
> the State and its people – have been sins also against Christ.[4]

This gets to the kernel of what is at issue here: the betrayal by
priests and bishops of Christ's example of love and selflessness
in an attempt to cling on to power and prestige.

This book will examine the implications of this betrayal for
the future of the Catholic Church in Ireland. What will emerge
in the wake of the findings of the Murphy Report? Has the
Church got any future in Ireland? Will it learn from previous
mistakes? Will it return to the simple origins of its founder, Jesus
of Nazareth? We have arrived at a crossroads and the future is
uncertain. Ronan Fanning remarks that the Murphy Report 'is a
truly historic landmark in the squalid history of Church-State relations' in Ireland. Looking back on the evolution of Catholicism
in the early decades of the new State, Fanning notes how pro-
Treaty and anti-Treaty forces were quite prepared to kill each
other in the pursuit of what constituted the legitimate State, but
that they 'made common cause in their unswerving allegiance to
the Catholic Church.' He adds:

> The political reality was that the craven deference of Irish
> politicians to the Catholic Church accurately reflected the no
> less craven deference of Irish voters, a deference that found its
> most disgusting manifestation in the revelation that some child
> victims of sexual abuse were punished by piously disbelieving
> parents for daring to say such things about the clergy.[5]

---

4. John Waters, 'The Church's sins are also sins against Christ. They re-
crucified Him', in *Irish Mail on Sunday*, 29 November 2009, p 27.
5. Ronan Fanning, 'The Age of our Craven Deference is finally over', in
The Sunday Independent, 6 December 2009, p 21.

Throughout the Murphy Report, we read of the embarrassment felt by the parents of the abused when they were forced to speak about what had happened to a bishop or some other official in the archdiocese. Fintan O'Toole thinks this is an illustration of how the Church had 'so successfully disabled a society's capacity to think for itself about right and wrong'. In effect, there had been a process of brainwashing so perverse that parents could express concern for the priest abuser, even when his victims happened to be their own children. O'Toole comes to the following conclusion:

> When all the numbing details of the report are absorbed, we have to reassemble the big picture of the institutional church's relationship with Irish society. And we have to say that relationship itself has been an abusive one. The church leadership behaved towards society with the same callousness, the same deviousness, the same exploitative mentality, and the same blindly egotistical pursuit of its own desires that an abuser shows towards his victim.[6]

The Church's fall from grace has been stunning in its rapidity and intensity. While numbers attending Mass and celebrating the sacraments are still high in Ireland by European standards, congregations to a large extent consist of middle-aged and older people. We are fast reaching the stage where there will be a massive scarcity of priests, given the age profile of those currently in active ministry. Also, the quality of the liturgy often leaves a lot to be desired, as do the music and the preaching. One wonders what will happen to the children and adolescents who are, to a large extent, unaware of the basic tenets of their Catholic faith, the 'unchurched', as Archbishop Martin described them soon after taking office in Dublin. These are presumably the future of the Church. How many of them will be inclined to practise a religion about which they know very little and which does not form an integral part of their lives?

Then there are those key issues with which the Church has had difficulties since they came to prominence in the 1960s: premarital and extramarital sex, homosexual behaviour, divorce,

6. Fintan O'Toole, 'Church relationship with Irish society has itself been abusive', in *The Irish Times*, 28 November 2009, p 15.

women priests, celibacy. In a revealing article in *The Irish Times*, Maureen Gaffney stated that very few Catholics look to the Church for guidelines in relation to any of these questions any more, which should not surprise us:

> After all, the church's teaching on sexuality continues to insist that all intentionally sought pleasure outside marriage is gravely sinful, and that every act of sexual intercourse within marriage must remain open to the transmission of life. The last pope, and most probably the present, took the view that intercourse, even in marriage, is not only 'incomplete', but even ceases to be an act of love, if contraception is used.[7]

An institution that continues to insist on teachings that are ignored by the vast majority of its own flock, risks losing all credibility. This lack of credibility is compounded when the Murphy Report has revealed how high-ranking officials in the Dublin Archdiocese moved known paedophiles from parish to parish, thus exposing more young people to abuse. Mervyn Rundle was abused by Fr Thomas Naughton, whose activities had been brought to the attention of the Church authorities years previously. Bishop Donal Murray failed to act on the complaints that were made against Naughton in 1983, which meant that Rundle and others were subjected to this priest's abuse. In an interview with Patsy McGarry, Rundle observed: 'My parents were shut out in the cold by the priests in the parish. They didn't want to know my parents anymore; they cut them dead. They were just vicious.'[8] Where is the evidence of Christian charity here? Why would members of the clergy turn against a family for bringing the abuse of their son to the attention of the authorities? Mervyn Rundle's family was not alone in encountering this attitude. Two of the contributors to this book, Marie Collins and Andrew Madden, were treated with contempt, disbelief and hostility when they revealed what had happened to them. A former seminarian, Ken Duggan, reported to the authori-

---

7. Maureen Gaffney, 'Church's view of sex the root cause of its troubles', in *The Irish Times*, 2 December 2009.
8. Patsy McGarry, 'Failure of Church to stop abuse led to suicides and settlements', in *The Irish Times*, 17 December 2009.

ties that a priest was abusing an altar boy (Andrew Madden) in the parish and assumed that action would be taken. It never happened. Duggan says of the episode:

> The whole experience of how they handled it was sickening. In a church which you studied for, you expect nothing but the highest of standards. You go naïvely, expecting your elders and the church to take action.[9]

One wonders if the survivors of abuse, as mentioned above, had not been so courageous, whether the general public would ever have learned about the extent of the problem in Dublin. Andrew Madden was the first person in Ireland to publicise his abuse by Fr Ivan Payne. What would have happened if he had chosen to remain silent? One thing we can say with certainty is that there would have been no rush on the part of the Church to deal with the problem adequately. Although people like Cardinal Desmond Connell claimed that the Church was largely ignorant of the nature of the illness of paedophilia, we now know that Church personnel were acutely aware of it for centuries, and also of the devious nature of those who were afflicted with the disease. They also knew enough about its prevalence among priests to insure the institution against the compensation claims by victims, which they realised would be inevitable as time went by. The Murphy Report has introduced a new *Realpolitik* with regard to the public's perception of the Church. The reaction of the Minister for Justice, Dermot Ahern, demonstrated the seismic shift in Irish political life when he declared that 'a collar will protect no criminal' and added: 'This is a republic – the people are sovereign – and no institution, no agency, no church can be immune from that fact.'[10] What a change is obvious here compared to the fate of Dr Noël Browne who, when faced with the bishops' disapproval of his Mother and Child Scheme, felt that he had no option but to resign as Minister for Health in 1951. Ahern was pointing out unambiguously that Ireland is a republic that is responsible for imple-

9. As quoted by Carl O'Brien 'Every day is like it happened yesterday', in *The Irish Times*, 27 November 2009, p 14.
10. '"A collar will protect no criminal", warns Minister for Justice', in *The Irish Times*, 27 November 2009, p 9.

menting the will of the people and that it must not allow any
interest group to exert undue influence on the affairs of State.
The poet Theo Dorgan sensed how significant the reaction to
Murphy has been:

> It seems very likely that something has changed forever in
> our republic. The skeletal presence of the Catholic Church in
> our institution and in our mores has begun to wither away,
> smoke in a gale, dust in the wind; there is a danger that with
> it will go the foundational ideals of justice, charity, compas-
> sion and mercy. We can already see the damage done in our
> country's short-lived flirtation with mammon. We have seen
> what happened when the post-Gorbachev USSR turned to
> gangster capitalism. We would do well to begin thinking
> clearly, and very soon, about what we will choose for the
> moral foundations of a post-Catholic Ireland.[11]

Dorgan raises a fundamental issue here – the importance of
finding a replacement for Catholicism's essential role in impress-
ing a moral code on Irish society. With its imminent demise as a
powerful force in Irish society, what remains to replace it? Have
the news media the capacity to take on such a function? One
would have to say that it is doubtful. What of the politicians?
Their image too has been seriously tainted in recent times. It is
highly unlikely that the institutional Church, if it survives, will
be able to supply the answers to the dilemmas facing Irish people at this important juncture. It may well be that individual
priests and religious sisters might come to the fore, or committed lay people who realise that the times we are living through
require a more proactive approach from them, or it may be individual politicians, writers, philanthropists, singers – people
with vision and the courage of their convictions. In a hard-hit-
ting editorial in the magazine *Reality*, Gerry Moloney pointed
out that something seems wrong when Church leaders 'appear
more interested in changing the language of the liturgy than trying to figure out why so many children were harmed by clerics.'
He continues that there is something dysfunctional when the

---

11. Theo Dorgan, 'Scandals could undermine the church's founda-
tions', in *The Irish Times*, 14 December 2009, p 14.

same Church seems more interested 'in silk robes and the Latin Mass and East-facing altars than in examining why our church has not been a safe environment for its most vulnerable members.' This is the kind of plain talking that is required in order to reach out to people. It is all the more impressive because it is rare to come across a priest who will write in such unambiguous terms about what is wrong in his Church. Writing in such a manner brings with it the risk of censure, the possibility of alienation among the clerical community as well as those Catholics who still remain unquestioningly faithful to a certain model of Church that has largely failed its followers. Moloney concludes:

> What we need is not a rigid, defensive, secretive church but an open, transparent, inclusive one; one where power and decision-making are not the preserve of elderly celibate males but where all the baptised – men and women, single and married, in ministry and outside it – are included and have a voice.[12]

If one were to ask Marie Collins and Andrew Madden what their experience of the Church has been, it would be a very far cry indeed from this idealised version. Both were brought up to respect the Church and its clergy. Both paid a very high price for that loyalty. It is unlikely that either could envisage an 'open', 'transparent', 'inclusive' Church emerging from the debris any time soon. Unless this ideal becomes a reality, however, unless a listening Church comes into being, one which truly embraces the poor and the downtrodden, those in pain as a result of marriage breakdown or sexual preference, those who happen to be female and want to remain within the Church in spite of all the discrimination they have endured through the decisions made by celibate males, unless there is evidence of genuine change, there has to be a serious question mark surrounding the future of the Catholic Church in Ireland.

This book may upset some people; it may anger others. As editors we make no apology for that. There has to be a forum where people can express their feelings freely and honestly about where the Catholic Church is headed in the aftermath of

---

12. Gerard Moloney, 'What kind of church?', in *Reality*, Volume 75, No 1, January 2010, p 5.

the Murphy Report. For healing to occur, there must be cathar-
sis; there must be a purgation of the passions. We are greatly in-
debted to our contributors for sharing their experiences in such
an honest and forthright manner. They do not all view the topic
in the same way. They may not always agree with the view-
points of other contributors or those of the editors. That is what
we intended. Whenever the opinions of people from diverse
backgrounds and experience are assembled on a topic as sensi-
tive as the Murphy Report, controversy and disagreement will
almost certainly ensue. All we can ask as editors is that contributors be honest in their opinions and true to the reality as they
perceive it. The various chapters you will read have the authentic
sound of a real hammer on a real anvil. The following inspir-
ational words from the prophetic priest-writer Jean Sulivan
(1913-1980), in his spiritual journal, *Morning Light* (1976), are
worthy of reflection. They have lost none of their resonance thirty
years after his death:

> The Church is something quite different than the guardian of
> a doctrine and a morality in the social sense of the word. It's
> that portion of humanity, visible or invisible, in which God,
> to the degree that images of his mythic representation were
> effaced, has found more space to advance than elsewhere –
> the God of the burning bush, of Abraham. It's the commu-
> nion of all those, neither the best nor the worst, whose gaze is
> focused on the far distance, who seem to be pointing to a
> human territory where the night is a little less dark and who
> help us believe that dawn will break in that direction.[13]

Such a model of Church is overdue in the Ireland of post-Murphy,
especially in the context of the revelations about Fr (now Cardinal)
Seán Brady's involvement in the 1975 Church investigations into
allegations of sexual abuse against Fr Brendan Smyth. What will
emerge from this incident, and from the Murphy Report, is not something that anyone can predict with certainty at the moment.

John Littleton
Eamon Maher

---

13. Jean Sulivan, *Morning Light: The Spiritual Journal of Jean Sulivan*, trs
Joseph Cunneen and Patrick Gormally (New York: Paulist Press, 1988),
p 156.

CHAPTER ONE

Come to Me all You who Labour[1]

Timothy Radcliffe OP

I thought that I would meditate on the text from Matthew which is all about resting: 'Come to me, all you who labour and are heavy laden, and I will give you rest. Take my yoke upon you, and learn from me; for I am gentle and lowly in heart, and you will find rest for your souls. For my yoke is easy and my burden is light.'

Jesus says to his disciples, 'Come to me.' It is an invitation to intimacy. They are invited to rest in his friendship. And that is what I want to explore a little. How in this tough time, we can rest in the Lord's friendship.

This is a terrible crisis for the Church, not just in Ireland, but in Britain, America and Australia. But I am convinced it is through crisis that we may grow close to God. The worst crisis that Israel ever knew was the destruction of the Temple and the monarchy and exile to Babylon in the sixth century BC. Israel lost everything that gave her identity: her worship, her nationhood, her king. But then she discovered God closer to her than ever before. God was present in the law, in their mouths and hearts, wherever they were, however far from Jerusalem. I was preparing this address on a Monday, and at midday office we sing, 'Your commands have been my delight; these I have loved. I will worship your commands and love them, and ponder your will.' They lost God only to receive him closer than they could have imagined.

And then that difficult man Jesus turned up, breaking the beloved law, eating on the Sabbath, touching the unclean, hanging out with prostitutes. He seemed to try to smash all that they loved, the very way that God was present in their lives. But that was only because God wished to be present even more intimately,

1. Edited extracts from this address to the priests of the Dublin Archdiocese were published in *The Tablet* on 18/26 December 2009 and 2 January 2010.

as one of us, with a human face. And at every Eucharist, we re-member how we had to lose him. But again only to receive him more closely, not as a man among us but as our very life.

This latest crisis is an opportunity to discover Jesus even closer to us than we had ever imagined. It is a crisis caused by our own failures as a Church, but God can make it a blessing, if we live it in faith. And so we can be calm. After I had been bang-ing on as usual about this, one of my American brethren made me a T-shirt: 'Have a good crisis.'

When I was a young Dominican student at Blackfriars, Oxford, the Priory was attacked by a right-wing group who re-sented our involvement in left-wing causes. They set off on dif-ferent nights two small explosives that made a lot of noise and blew in the windows. It woke up the whole community except the Prior. I was fascinated to discover what the brethren wore in bed! Pyjamas, boxer shorts, nothing! The police and the fire brigade came around. Finally I went to wake the Prior. 'Fergus, the Priory has been attacked, wake up.' 'Is anyone dead?' 'No.' 'Is anybody wounded?' 'No.' 'Well, let me sleep and we will think about it in the morning.' That was my first lesson in lead-ership! Christ has won the victory. We can be calm whatever happens.

So the question for us today is: How can we live this crisis as a time of blessing and new life. Let's carry on looking at what Jesus says, and see what it suggests: 'Come to me, all you who labour and are heavy laden and I will give you rest.'

In the past while, most of us have probably been feeling pretty heavy laden. We may be weighed down with the burden of the scandal of abuse; with the failure of many bishops to face this over decades. We may feel crushed by the anger of the press, the anger of some parishioners, and perhaps even worse their sad, sympathetic disappointment. Whenever I give lectures in England these days I come away exhausted with the anger against the Church.

How can we bring this to the Lord so that he can take the weight off our shoulders? Well, he says 'come to me all you who are heavy burdened.' ALL YOU. That means that we come to him together with all of those who are weighed down. We have to go to him with those who carry the heaviest burdens of all, the abused. If we are to grow closer to Jesus, then we have to help them with their burden. That looks like an additional burden, but eventually it will take a weight off our shoulders too.

I admit that I am afraid of that. I fear the anger and the hurt of those we have abused. When I hear them talk on the radio or TV I can barely cope. I want to turn it off. But friendship with the Lord implies that we must stagger along, somehow, bearing their burden, and their anger and their hurt. And the disappointment and sorrow of the people of God. And even the heavy burdens of our fellow priests who abused minors. We must help them to carry their burden. If we carry each other's burdens, then the Lord will give us rest.

At the Last Supper in Luke's gospel, Jesus says to the disciples: 'For I tell you that this scripture must be fulfilled in me, "And he was reckoned with the transgressors"; for what is written about me has its fulfilment' (22:37).

If we are to rest in the friendship of Jesus, then we shall probably find ourselves numbered among the transgressors. A wonderful Irish Dominican sister told me that she went to a vast family reunion, hundreds of relatives. And there was a vast family tree, and under each name, a list of their descendants. And under her name and that of a priest cousin, was a '?'. As if to say, 'Well, we do not know what you have been up to.' Once in New York, the local provincial asked me to meet a man who claimed to have been abused by a Dominican who was long since dead. I had a harrowing hour with him and his wife as he shouted, in effect, 'You did it.' We were exactly the same age. I had never even heard of the Dominicans then. I was tempted to shout out, 'But it was nothing to do with me.' And it is tempting to reach for comforting facts, such as that in the USA and in England, surveys have shown that actually other clergy tend to offend more often than Catholic priests, although we get all the flak.

One way in which we can rest is by throwing off the heavy burden of being righteous. It is so tiring having to pretend to be a saint all the time. The saints often talk about what terrible sinners they are, and this often seemed to me to be crazy! How pretentious! But, of course, they knew their solidarity with the mass of ordinary sinners.

Archbishop Rembert Weakland, who had to resign because of a scandal that involved sex and money, wrote in his autobiography of the sort of release that the crisis gave him. He remarked that St Thérèse of Lisieux 'once wrote that she wanted to go to God empty handed. I think I know now personally what she meant by that phrase. I have learned how frail my own human nature is, how in need of God's loving embrace I am.'[2]

H. G. Wells wrote a short story about the Last Judgement. A terrible sinner, King Ahab, Elijah's old opponent, is placed in the palm of God for judgement. And he squeals and tries to flee as the recording angel reads out all of his sins, until finally he flees up God's sleeve and finds refuge. And then a saintly prophet comes, probably Elijah, and he sits in the palm of God too and listens complacently as his good deeds are read out. And then the recording angel gets to some unsavoury stuff: 'It seemed not ten seconds before the saint also was rushing to and fro over the great palm of God. Not ten seconds. And at last he also shrieked beneath that pitiless and cynical exposition (of the recording angel), and fled also, even as the wicked man had fled, into the shadow of the sleeve. And the two sat side by side, stark of all delusion, in the shadow of the robe of God's charity, like brothers. And thither also I fled in my turn.'

So let us bear each other's burdens, of the victims, the abusers, the people of God. Let us cast off the heavy burden of trying to shore up our righteousness and find rest up God's sleeve, with all the other poor sods.

'Take my yoke upon you and learn from me ... For my yoke is easy and my burden is light.'
This yoke of Jesus is his Law. In the Old Testament (Sir 51:26) and rabbinic Judaism, the Torah was the yoke that was laid upon us. And the contrast is with the Pharisees who 'bind heavy burdens, hard to bear, and lay them on people's shoulders, but they themselves will not move them with their finger' (23:4). Unlike the Pharisees, the yoke of Jesus is light.

If we think about our own beloved Church in recent centuries, then we seem to have been more like Pharisees, laying

2. *A Pilgrim in a Pilgrim Church: Memoirs of a Catholic Archbishop* (William Eerdmans Publishing Co, 2009), p 5.

heavy burdens on the shoulders of the people. Often this has been associated with sexual behaviour. We have told families with large numbers of children that no contraception is permitted, and young people who cannot afford to get married that their sexual behaviour must be strictly controlled – no more than ten seconds for a kiss – and gay people that nothing is permitted and that they should be ashamed of their sexuality. Now, regardless of the rights or wrongs of Church teaching, this has been experienced by our people as a heavy burden. And then they discover that priests who have been weighing them down have been sinning sexually in a far more grievous manner. Like the Pharisees, not practising what we preach. You can imagine the anger of a woman who has had child after child and can bear no more, or a young gay person, when they hear what even a few priests have been up to!

And that anger is all the more exacerbated because paedophilia has become *the* sexual sin. In a secular society like England, there really aren't any others anymore. On the recent BBC programme *The Moral Maze*, they discussed the woman known as Belle de Jour, who got herself through her doctoral studies by becoming a part-time prostitute. Most of the panel could see nothing wrong with that. It was just a contractual relationship. We can do what we want with our bodies. And isn't sado-masochism just one of the rich tapestry of sexual experiences? For some strange reason, it seems attractive for the English upper classes. So all that disquiet about sexual behaviour, all that sense that something is going wrong, all that anxiety becomes focused on the paedophile. He or she is the great sexual sinner, the only sinner. I do not want in any way to play down the seriousness of the offence, which is indeed horrible and inexcusable, but to help understand the degree of intense anger. Sexual abuse of minors is, I suspect, the lightening rod for all our anxieties about sexuality and about how it seems to have become detached from any moral vision.

So how are we to lighten the burden on other people and on ourselves? How can Jesus teach how to share his yoke which is easy and light? Of course we must be kind and compassionate with other people and with ourselves. I would guess that the great majority of priests are that. Though my so-called Irish

brother, Herbert McCabe, did tell me that once he went to confession in Dublin and was given a terrible blowing up. He went
out of the confessional, said his penance, waited until the priest
emerged and then gave him an even worse rocket.

But we need something much more radical than kindness.
We need a renewed understanding of what it means to bear the
yoke of Jesus' commandments. We have to challenge this whole
idea that morality is mainly about prohibitions and obligations.
The idea that being good is a matter of submitting one's will to
the Great Policeman in the sky is late and mistaken. Some people
put the blame on Ockham, but far be it for me as a Dominican to
point the finger at one of my Franciscan brothers! I believe that
this moral vision certainly took over during the Enlightenment
with its culture of control. It saw the world and society as a
mechanism which must be controlled, like a clock. And the
moral laws were the will of the clockmaker. Being good is the
submission to the arbitrary will of God and of the State. It is
about what you are allowed to do and what is forbidden.

We have to relieve everyone, including ourselves, of this
heavy burden of the Celestial Policeman. The Ten Commandments were not originally seen either in Israel or the early
Church as God's arbitrary will. If we do, then some of us may
sympathise with Bertrand Russell when he said that they should
be thought of as an examination paper: No candidate should attempt more than six! There was a Polish Dominican chaplain in
the Second World War. On the eve of the battle of Monte Casino,
he opened his tent and was alarmed to see thousands of Polish
soldiers wanting to confess. What could he do? This was before
general absolution was thought of, let alone forbidden. And so
he got them all to lie face down, so that no one could see anyone
else. And he said, 'I will go through the Ten Commandments. If
you have broken one, waggle your left foot and with your right
indicate how many times.'

I had a fascinating conversation with the Chief Rabbi of
Great Britain, Jonathan Sachs, this summer. He told me that in
the Torah there is no word for 'to obey', in the sense of submission of your will to external control. When the State of Israel was
founded after the last World War, they needed to borrow a
word from Aramaic for 'obey' in this modern sense. Instead the

Hebrew word which we usually translate as 'obey' means 'to listen.' The commandments are not an external constraint. They
are always an invitation to enter a personal relationship with
God. 'I am the Lord your God, who brought you out of the land
of Egypt, out of the house of bondage. You shall have no other
gods before me' (Ex 20:2f). The Ten Commandments are sharing
in God's friendship and freedom. They are given to Moses, to
whom God spoke as to a friend.

And so it is with Jesus. Jesus revealed his new commandment to the disciples on the night before he died, at exactly the
moment that he claimed them as his friends. 'I have called you
friends, for all that I have heard from my Father I have made
known to you' (Jn 15:15).

This explains something really puzzling about Jesus. He ate
and drank with prostitutes and tax collectors; he had the most
disreputable friends. He did not wait until they had repented
before he invited them to the table. He did not say, 'Look
Joanna, once you have been off the street for a week, you can
come to my party.' He just accepted them as they were. And yet
he preached the Sermon on the Mount. He commanded his disciples to turn the other cheek, to love their enemies, never to be
angry, to be perfect as our Heavenly Father is perfect. He was
very demanding.

How could he do all of these things, be unreservedly welcoming, apparently lax, and very demanding? The exigencies
were those of God's friendship. It is only in the visible context of
friendship that we can give moral teaching.

Now this has radical consequences for how the Church
teaches a moral vision. What we have to say only makes sense in
the context of friendship. If we want to speak on questions like
abortion, or divorce and remarriage, or the gay issue, then we
must be seen to be the friends of these people. We must accept
their hospitality and invite them into our homes. When I was a
student in Paris, Cardinal Daniélou died on the staircase, visit-
ing a prostitute. The press was filled with salacious innuendos.
But everyone who knew the Cardinal understood that he was a
holy man who was carrying out his pastoral care of the despised, as he had always done. He was offering friendship to the
despised.

So this yoke of Jesus is easy and his burden is light because it
is the offer of his friendship, and it can only be communicated in
friendship. Indeed what is to be said can only be discovered in
friendship. It is only side by side, sharing the struggle and the
search, that we will be given the right word. And this word can
never be burden, only a gift.

This will be terribly difficult to communicate to the media.
They want nice clear statements, preferably forbidding things.
But then the newspapers are a typical product of the Enlightenment and its culture of control. And this brings us to another
way in which Jesus teaches us how to rest and be at peace.

'For I am gentle and lowly in heart, and you will find rest for your souls.'
Friendship with Jesus, intimacy, means learning to be gentle
and lowly of hearts. Then we shall find rest for our souls. But I
am not sure that if one thinks of the Catholic Church the first
word that springs to mind will be humble. Indeed I do not think
that it is characteristic of any Church that I know. I once attended
an ecumenical meeting in Bari and a very grand archbishop of
another Church came up to me, dressed in glory. And he asked
me what titles I bore: Your Serenity? Your Beatitude? Your
Magnificence? In a moment of naughtiness, I said that if the
brethren wanted to be very formal, they could call me 'brother'.
And then he asked what were the symbols of my authority as
Master of the Order. Did I have a special hat? A crozier? And
when I replied that I had none at all he walked away thinking
that clearly I was not worth talking to.

I am convinced that this whole sexual crisis is deeply linked
with power and the way power often works in the Church at all
levels, from the Vatican to the parish sacristan. It is not the
power of Jesus, who was gentle and lowly of heart. Every
human institution revolves around the use of power. I do believe
that with that the Enlightenment culture of control, our obsession with power has deepened. Charles Taylor, in his wonderful
book *A Secular Age*, traces the evolution of claims for ever
greater power. We see the rise of absolute monarchs in England,
France and Spain, the development of the centralised state. The
poor cease to be seen as our brothers and sisters in Christ and
become a threat. They must be locked up, like the mentally ill.

We have standing armies and the establishment of police forces, and the explosion of legislation.

The Church, alas, has often been infected by this same culture of control. I am reminded of the bishop who said, 'Everyone in this diocese is equal, from me downwards.' And another who at his consecration promised to serve the diocese with a rod of iron!

I suspect that this happened partly because the Church has for centuries been struggling to defend itself against the powers of this world who want to take it over. From the Roman Empire until the Communist Empires, passing by the British Empire and others, the Church has struggled to keep hold of its own life, and often ended up marked with the same culture of power. And it is this same culture of power that lies at the root of the crisis of sexual abuse, which is the abuse of power over the small and vulnerable.

We will not have a Church which is safe for the young until we learn from Christ and become again a humble Church in which we are equal children of the one Father. Then Christ will give rest for our souls.

In the Office of Readings for the first week of Advent, there is a wonderful reading from Isaiah. It was born of the experience of crisis and humiliation that his people were living through. But for Isaiah, it promised that they would again share God's own life and peace:

> For the Lord of hosts has a day against all that is proud and lofty, against all that is lifted up and high; against all the cedars of Lebanon, lofty and lifted high, against all the high mountains, and against all the lofty hills, against every high tower and against every fortified wall. (Is 2:12-15)

> Then the Lord will create over the whole site of Mountain and over her assemblies a cloud by day and smoke and the shining of a flaming fire by night; for all over the glory there will be a canopy and a pavilion. It will be a shade by day from the heart and for a refuge and a shelter from the storm and rain. (4:5-6).

This is a terrible crisis for the Church, but it carries a promise and a blessing, if we accept it. It is much more than the crisis of the sexual abuse of minors by some priests and religious. It is the crisis of a whole understanding of priesthood and religious life. The Reformation was a response to the crisis of the late Middle Ages. We had a priesthood entirely unable to cope with a new world. The clergy were largely uneducated, hardly able to celebrate the Mass, often with concubines. Even the religious were pretty dubious. There was a Spanish saying: 'Never trust a Jesuit with your wallet. Never trust a friar with your wife.'

That crisis led to an extraordinary renewal of the priesthood, with a new spirituality, new seminaries, a more profound theological formation, a new discipline. But often it gave the impression that we were sexual eunuchs, asexual beings. Children speculated as to whether nuns had legs under those long habits or glided around on wheels. Once when I was preaching in the open air, standing on a soap box, I heard a child say to his mother: 'Mummy, why is that man wearing a skirt?' Then a small hand lifted the bottom of my habit: 'It's alright Mummy. He's got trousers on underneath.'

We are living through the crisis of that whole understanding of priesthood, with its remoteness from people, with its use of power, with its understanding of morality in terms of control. Painfully, the Lord is demolishing our high towers and our pretentions to glory and grandeur so that he can make his home with us.

The vast majority of priests and bishops that I have met around the world are humble and unpretentious people, who only want to serve the people of God. Most priests that I know want to share the life of their people and are at their beck and call. Ever since I began to travel around the Church, I have been deeply edified. And I have the same impression of so many priests. You can be very proud of your humility. But often it is all the more impressive because it flies in the face of structures and traditions which would lift us up and make us lofty, bestow on us grand titles, extraordinary clothes. And so this crisis may be the beginning of a wonderful renewal of the Church, in which we shall indeed learn from Jesus, 'for I am gentle and lowly in heart, and you will find rest for your souls'.

The final word which I leave with you is 'rest'. Jesus said to his disciples when they were exhausted, 'Come aside and rest awhile.' And I hope you will be restful, and that you will resist the temptation to be checking your emails every ten seconds and rushing around with your mobile phones.

We can only offer people the promise of Christ's rest if we are seen to be people who enjoy it sometimes ourselves. Priests often are overactive anyway, but this crisis can exacerbate that tendency. We may feel that we have to show that we are exceptionally good priests, constantly serving the people and without a second for ourselves. That is salvation by works and not by grace.

Thomas Merton believed that to be overactive was to collude with the violence of our society: 'The rush and pressure of modern life are a form, perhaps the most common form, of its innate violence. To allow oneself to be carried away by a multitude of conflicting concerns, to surrender to too many demands, to commit oneself to too many projects, to want to help everyone in everything is to succumb to violence. More than that, it is cooperation in violence. The frenzy of the activist neutralises his own inner capacity for peace. It destroys the fruitfulness of his own work, because it kills the roots of inner wisdom which makes work fruitful.'

If that activism does violence to us, then it will succeed somehow. We may find that we are speaking violent words to other people. We may do violence to ourselves through drink or drugs. We may even become sexually violent, especially to the vulnerable.

And so we need, without shame, to rest in God. And the passage from Matthew at the beginning of this chapter suggests some of the ways in which we can do this.

We can rest because this crisis can be fruitful. It may be a time of new blessing and a renewal of the Church. We can face it calmly because the victory is won. Christ has died; Christ is risen; Christ will come again. As Dietrich Bonhoeffer said to his fiend, the Bishop of Chichester, before he was murdered by the Nazis: 'The victory is certain.'

We can rest because we do not have to pretend that, unlike those awful priests, we are terribly good. We drop the heavy burden of the pious mask and flee up God's sleeve.

We can rest because Jesus' yoke is light. His commandments

are the invitation to friendship. Friendship may be demanding, but it is never a burden.

And we can let go of all the heavy weight of being important and powerful people.

CHAPTER TWO

A Church Disgraced

Andrew Madden

The Dublin Archdiocese's pre-occupations in dealing with cases of child sexual abuse, at least until the mid 1990s, were the maintenance of secrecy, the avoidance of scandal, the protection of the reputation of the Church, and the preseveration of its assets. All other considerations, including the welfare of children and justice for victims, were subordinated to these priorities. (Murphy Report, Paragraph 1.15)

By 10.00am on the morning of Thursday 26 November 2009 I was sitting in a room in a building owned by the Department of Justice on Harcourt Street in the city centre. Also there were Maeve Lewis and Ruth Carroll from the support organisation One-In-Four, and Marie Collins, who was also sexually abused by a Catholic priest in Dublin when she was a child. The Murphy Report was to be published at 2.15pm and we were being given an opportunity to read it in advance. I had asked the Justice Minister, Dermot Ahern, to provide me with an embargoed copy twenty four hours in advance of publication, but he declined. In another building nearby, many journalists were locked into a room and availing of the same opportunity.

As Maeve, Ruth, Marie and I were each given our own copies of the Report we fell silent and starting reading. Some months earlier I had had an opportunity to read the chapter on Father Ivan Payne who had sexually abused me as a child and I immediately sought it out to read it again. The language and the clarity with which the Report was written meant nearly every sentence had an impact. 'Ivan Payne is a convicted serial child sexual abuser', it said. No matter how many times I read that, it still shocks me that such a person walked into my life when I was only eleven years of age; the impact was always going to be huge. For me that impact came very soon after, for him it would come many years later.

I was so saddened to see, there on the page, in black and white, that at least seven more young boys were sexually abused by Ivan Payne after I had complained about him in 1981. My school teacher, Ken Duggan, had gone to Archbishop's House on my behalf and told Monsignor Alex Stenson that I had said that Ivan Payne had molested me on a weekly basis for about two and a half years. Many weeks later word came back that Ivan Payne had accepted my allegations as being true; if the Catholic Church in Dublin had removed Ivan Payne from ministry at that point, he would never have met those other boys. Instead they assigned him to a new parish in Sutton and he continued sexually abusing children. So many young lives were damaged by a priest who the Catholic Church knew molested children.

I was shocked by the repport about Bishop O'Mahony's behaviour. How had he secured a medical report to the effect that it was safe to reassign Ivan Payne? He told the psychiatrist that a complaint had been received from a seventeen-year-old but he didn't tell him that the behaviour complained of took place at a time when the seventeen-year-old was between twelve and fourteen years of age. As I began to read the other chapters, I was further shocked at Bishop O'Mahony's similar behaviour in handling allegations against other priests.

The more I read, the sadder and angrier I became. I felt so sad for the nine-year-old girl who had to endure the priest putting his hands inside her trousers during confession so as to abuse her and then washing his hands in an altar bowl afterwards. And this, four years after the first complaint had been received about him: such inadequate dereliction of duty made me angry. I felt sad for the boys who, as grown men, felt guilty that they had not complained about their abuser earlier because, if they had done so, other children might have been saved from similar abuse. I became angry for those men carrying a guilt that wasn't theirs to carry and even more annoyed that their concern for other children was not matched by the bishops, who moved the same priest time and time again as he abused children from 1950 to 1979.

I looked at the Report in my hands: seven hundred and fifty pages, three decades. So many children sexually abused by priests and so much of that abuse covered up by the Catholic Church in Dublin. I thought about my journey to get to this stage. Going public in 1995, letting people know that I had been compensated in 1993 by a priest who was still in active ministry in a Dublin parish fourteen years after I had first reported him. Participating in the criminal proceedings against Ivan Payne which led to his conviction in 1998 for sexually abusing ten boys. Asking the then Taoiseach, Bertie Ahern, over ten years ago to have an inquiry into the Catholic Church and being shocked by his response that such an inquiry could only be held into 'matters of urgent public importance'. The Catholic Church in Dublin subordinated the welfare of children to its own priorities, and they had a like-minded ally in Mr Ahern. More vulnerable children paid the price – a dreadful indictment of a system of cover up and collusion.

By the time I left the Department of Justice shortly after midday I was both deeply saddened and furiously angry. I went out to RTÉ to pre-record a piece for *Prime Time* later that night and the emotion showed: there was just too much of it to keep it under wraps.

Later that day and over the next few days my reaction to the Report was mixed with my feelings as I watched other people's reactions. I listened to Archbishop Martin's speech at the Mater Dei Institute. Very emotional. Very clever. He expressed sadness for the poor victims, horror at the awful paedophile priests. No mention of his Church's cover up and the further sexual abuse of children that it caused – this was what the Murphy Report was really about. The man who hadn't put a foot wrong since he became Archbishop of Dublin had started a process of damage limitation and self-preservation for his Church. I felt that this was not the proper way to respond to the Report. The next morning I was on a radio programme with Bishop Eamonn Walsh; what did he have to say about seven hundred and fifty pages of bishops covering up for priests who had sexually abused children over a thirty-year period, a group that only constituted a representative sample of both the allegations and the cover up? None of this was deliberate he claimed; in other words, the same 'mistake' repeated over and over again for thirty years was a complete accident. I was furious that the process of minimising the contents of the Report was underway so quickly, or indeed that it should have begun at all. Where was the acknowledgement of their own part in all of this? Where were the signs of their humility and sadness? And indeed where was the anger they should have had at themselves for what they had done?

There was more. No need, Bishop Walsh said, to have the Commission of Investigation look into other dioceses around the country – after all, taxpayers' resources were tight. Neither Bishop Walsh nor any of his fellow bishops were concerned about taxpayers' resources when they were used to pay for the Ferns Inquiry, the Child Abuse Commission, the Redress Board or the Dublin Inquiry. Bishop Walsh's new-found concern for taxpayers' resources was only conveniently kicking in now that we who had been abused had succeeded in having the full truth about Dublin exposed and wanted the same for people who had been abused in other parts of the country. The same pattern continued over the weekend with Archbishop Martin saying on RTÉ Radio on Sunday lunchtime that the other bishops who had been working as bishops in Dublin during any of the period 1975-2004 were entitled to a fair hearing. This implied that those bishops (Donal Murray, James Moriarty, Raymond Field, Eamonn Walsh and Martin Drennan) had not had a fair hearing to date, another attempt to undermine the Commission of Investigation. They needed to answer the questions raised by the Report, the Archbishop said. What Martin was conveniently overlooking was the fact that the Report doesn't ask questions, it makes findings, findings of fact, which are found at the end of each chapter.

I was so angry that the Catholic Church could so brazenly attempt to put up a fight against a report that should have brought it to its knees in shame. The arrogance was contemptible. By now calls were well under way for all currently serving bishops who had been part of a structure within the Archdiocese of Dublin which had facilitated the cover up of the sexual abuse of children to resign. Astonishingly, none of them thought they should have to. Each of them fought to hold onto power and privilege. They seemed to have looked through the sections of the Report which identified them and decided the content wasn't sufficiently strong to bring about their resignation. There was no connection between the awfulness of the content of the Report and the emotionless self-serving responses of the bishops.

Bishop Moriarty said he was not directly criticised in the Report, Bishop Drennan said there was nothing negative about him either, Bishop Field said he'd done nothing wrong, Bishop Walsh said if he had done any wrong he'd be gone and Bishop Murray said he never deliberately or knowingly sought to cover up or withhold information brought to his attention. None of them seemed to be at all affected by the horror of the experiences so many children had at the hands of priests they had responsibility for. Didn't they care? No, they didn't. Paragraph 1.35 of the Report describes the bishops' attitude: 'There was little or no concern for the welfare of the abused child or for the welfare of other children who might come into contact with the priest.' Judging from the behaviour of the bishops as they obscenely attempted to cling onto office, they had no more concern for the welfare of adult men and women who demanded they account and take responsibility for what they had done, and what they had failed to do, as they had for those same men and women when they were little children whose lives were being devastated by known paedophile priests.

Former Taoiseach, Bertie Ahern, never put the welfare of children before the welfare of the Catholic vote, but what about his successor, Mr Cowen? Four days after the Report was published what was his response to one priest abusing over a hundred children, another priest abusing children on a fortnightly basis for twenty five years, another priest inserting a crucifix into one girl's vagina and back passage, the same priest subsequently appointed to a hospital which gave him access to more children, a naked priest swimming with naked children in the swimming pool in his garden, another priest with a violent and aggressive history knocking a boy unconscious before being moved to the Diocese of San Diego with a reference from Archbishop Connell to the effect that he was 'an excellent priest in many ways' and 'a priest in good standing'? Every Archbishop from McQuaid to Connell knew, many auxiliary bishops knew, and the vast majority of priests who were aware of particular instances of abuse simply chose to turn a blind eye. Taoiseach Cowen's response? 'It's a crushing indictment, em, in terms of where the good name and standing of an institution was put above the, eh, importance of the safety of the children as the primary objective and I think that I'd emphasise that it's very important that people would know that the Gardaí are available to investigate any allegation that people may have.' He might as well have been talking about NAMA (National Assets Management Agency). And his response to the question of the bishops who covered up these crimes against children staying on as the patrons of most of the national schools in their dioceses? Cowen: 'In respect of em, the appropriateness of people holding office, ecclesiastical office, that has to be a matter for those institutions.'

What sort of a country do I live in? The political leader (albeit with no mandate) of the country thinks it should be left to the same institution whose structures and rules facilitated the cover up of the sexual abuse of children (Paragraph 1.113) to decide if the same bishops whose actions caused the further sexual abuse of children should be allowed to stay in office. Not one thought for the needs of those who had been sexually abused for accountability. Not one thought for the welfare of children in schools managed by that same institution. Not one thought for the parents who didn't want their children confirmed by bishops who had covered up for paedophile priests. Not one notion as to what it is to be the leader of a country. I was furious that the same deference Ahern was showing to the Catholic Church in 1998 by refusing to have them investigated was being matched by Cowen now that the Report had been published.

Can the Catholic Church in Ireland survive all of this? Undoubtedly. They have the leader of our country in our national parliament bending the knee in their direction within a week of reading (presuming he bothered) a report into how they covered up the rape and sexual abuse of children for thirty years. They have their priests. Those poor priests whose good work we hear so much about. Working away at the coalface in despair at the way their bishops have let them down – except of course they are not in despair. They had little to say when Cardinal Connell tried to block the Commission of Investigation from having access to the files it needed to uncover the truth. They have never spoken collectively in support of a single victim at any time in the last fifteen years that child sexual abuse by priests has been in the public domain. Yet note how they raised

their heads above the parapet to support Bishop Murray in
Limerick and Bishop Drennan in Galway. Both bishops were
happy to announce they enjoyed the full support of their priests.
Had any of these priests been sexually abused by a priest in
Dublin as a child? Had any of them watched a family member's
life disintegrate over many years because they were abused as a
child by a priest? Had any of these priests had to live with guilt
that wasn't theirs, like so many parents have had to do, because
they insisted their children participated in church-related activities which gave paedophile priests easy access to them? Had
any of these priests cried themselves to sleep at night for years
because they hadn't noticed anything wrong with their children
when they were being abused, and now can't forgive themselves? Yes, the Catholic Church has the support of its poor, unfortunate priests and they are welcome to it. What the Church
and its priests have lost is any claim to moral authority, but such
is their collective arrogance don't expect to notice any time soon.

They will survive too with the support of 'the faithful'. Mass-
going Catholics who contact radio programmes I'm contributing to and voice support for their inexcusable bishop and then
say no, they haven't read the Report and they don't know what
he's 'supposed to have done'. Mass-going Catholics who ignore
camera crews outside churches, declining invitations to respond
to the Murphy Report, emerge only weeks later to so articulately
express their unbearable sadness at the sight of burnt-out
Longford Cathedral. Mass-going Catholics who march up and
down outside 'sexshops', objecting to them opening up in their
areas and then march into Mass the Sunday after the Murphy
Report was published with not a scintilla of embarrassment
about their sickening hypocrisy.

The Catholic Church continues to enjoy a lot of power it
should not have in a modern republican democracy. Priests,
bishops and nuns sit on the boards of hospitals and use ethics
committees to maintain a Catholic ethos within publicly funded
services with no regard for the religious views of people paying
for and using those services. In my country I would prefer to see
public ownership of publicly-funded services including hospi
tals and schools. When I attend a hospital paid for out of public
funds, to which I have contributed, I want my treatment deter-

mined by my medical need, not by other people's religious views. Similarly I think it inappropriate that publicly-funded schools should have an enrolment policy which gives preference to children with baptismal certificates. Schools may have a different ethos in terms of religious instruction, but the State should be the patron of all publicly-funded schools and should be responsible for the safety, welfare and protection of children in such establishments, and should be recognised as the employer of all school staff, including teachers.

Thankfully, since publication of the Ryan and Murphy Reports in 2009, a huge public debate is taking place in Ireland about the role the Catholic Church has in our society and what, if anything, we want to do to change it. I am absolutely sure the relationship between Fianna Fáil and the Catholic Church has not served this country well, certainly not from what I have observed since Fianna Fáil came to power in 1997. They have served each other well and we have paid the price. That situation is unacceptable to me and I intend to play my part in bringing about change. I want much higher standards of child protection in this country and I want to see at least one person in the Oireachtas whose *sole priority* every single day is the safety, welfare and protection of our children.

CHAPTER THREE

Sacred Heart, Sacred Mind: The Challenge of Conviction in the Catholic Church

Colum Kenny

Cor Jesu, flagrans amore hominum, Venite adoremus![1]

The image was often found in Catholic homes. It has hung in many Irish kitchens. A benign and white-skinned Jesus gazes softly out, his raised right hand bestowing a blessing. Flames and light emanate from his pierced heart. In some houses stood a small statue, with the sacred heart of Jesus likewise visible at the centre of its chest. In front of the picture or statue glowed a little cross inside red glass, the direct wiring of which was a popular option offered by fitters to customers of Ireland's earliest rural electrification schemes.

The image fell out of general favour during the last four decades of the twentieth century. Many today regard it, at best, as sentimental[2] 'kitsch'. We are embarrassed by the faith of our ancestors. We do not go as far as the young and rebellious surrealist painter, Salvidor Dalí (1904-89) who, after his beloved mother had died eight years earlier, exhibited in 1929 an outline of the Sacred Heart upon which he scrawled, *'Parfois je crache par plaisir sur le portrait de ma mère* (Sometimes I spit for pleasure on the portrait of my mother)'.[3] Nevertheless, the Sacred Heart now speaks to many not of love but of naïvety or even superstition. It is associated with an age of seemingly simple faith but not so simple sexual abuse, violence, ignorance and institutional corruption as revealed in the Murphy Report and elsewhere.

And yet what was it about that image that once so endeared

1. 'Adoration', at Hieronymus Noldin, *The Devotion to the Sacred Heart of Jesus* (New York, 1905), pp 251-4.
2. E. M. Catich, 'Sentimentality in Christian art', in *The Furrow*, 10 (8) (1959), pp 504, 512-4.
3. Fèlix Fanés, *Salvador Dalí: The Construction of the Image, 1925-30* (Yale, 2007), pp 153-7.

it to people? It was the call of compassion, the identification of a force that was felt to enrich daily life, the visualisation of a fire and light emanating from the gospels. That, and also the consolation of being loved as a species, of daring to believe that we are born for meaning rather than by chance. The first Friday of each month became a time of special spiritual observation for those inspired by the Sacred Heart.

If our ancestors were deluding themselves by such devotion then they were doing so in a way that was recognised as exquisite by Elizabeth Barrett Browning (1806-61), who wistfully compared such experiences to the highest feelings of human love. She declared to her future husband: 'I love thee with a love I seemed to lose / With my lost saints'.[4] The fact that Elizabeth regarded her love for Robert Browning as being of the same quality or type as that which she had once felt for certain saints is an indication of the complex psychological relationship between love and desire, between yearning in general and sexuality. The exercise of power was undoubtedly a key factor in the situations examined by Judge Murphy, but confusion over sex and sexuality also has an important place in the pathology of abuse within Catholicism. While being cautious not to jump to facile or offensive conclusions about the consequences of celibacy, and not to equate acts of devotion or sacrifice with the surrender implicit in sexual intercourse, Christians as much as anyone should be aware of the dangers of unconsciously sublimating or repressing sexual energies. The French psychoanalyst Jacques Lacan cautioned against simplification in such matters when he said:

> Sublimation may be at work in the 'oblation' that radiates from love, but we should try to go a little further into the structure of the sublime and not confuse it with the perfect orgasm – an equation Freud, in any case, opposed.
>
> The worse thing is that the souls who overflow with the most natural tenderness are led to wonder whether they satisfy the delusional normalism of the genital relation – an unheralded burden that we have loaded onto the shoulders of the innocent ...[5]

4. From *Sonnets from the Portuguese*, Number 43.
5. Lacan, *Écrits*, trs Bruce Fink (New York, 2006), p 507.

The term 'delusional normalism' is surely one that may be applied to that Irish society which was blind to the sexual abuse of children. Its very terror of physical desire was part of the problem. In this context, among others, the image of the pumping, material organ represented as the Sacred Heart of Jesus serves to remind us that there is no sacred existence without an integration of the body, mind and soul. Perhaps our ancestors, and those many priests or nuns who did 'overflow with the most natural tenderness' and who had no part in child sexual abuse or its cover-up, were attracted to the image of the Sacred Heart by its implicit groundedness. The part stood for the whole.

We may consider ourselves today to be more sophisticated than our ancestors, but it is arrogant to assume that we are more intelligent. And it is not intelligent to dismiss devotional practices as simply self-deception. Devotion to a mature teacher, and the visualisation of compassionate energy, can be a fruitful spiritual practice with positive personal and social outcomes.

When faith is founded on experiential realities such as compassion, and on intellectual convictions, it is firm. For centuries, the form of faith represented by the Catholic Church was not just devotionally satisfactory but resonated as a set of explanations and ideals that persuaded Irish people to remain loyal to that institution. No doubt the politics of Anglo-Irish affairs from the Reformation onwards reinforced such loyalty but, in Ireland and elsewhere, there was also a scholarly and monastic tradition within Catholicism of which people were aware and proud.

What has changed has not just been the status of the hierarchy, damaged by the mishandling of child sexual abuse complaints. The abuse scandal, woeful and all as it has been, does not fully explain a falling away from the faith of our fathers and mothers. It is as if a generation awoke from a dream, bewildered by the sexual violence that had been perpetrated against children and broken hearted to learn from both media and the legal system that perpetrators had been sheltered from justice by people who purported to represent Christ on earth. The failure of the hierarchy and other authorities to deal appropriately with criminality compounded for some of the laity a gradual weakening of their confidence in the institutional Church and its teachings. To them, the Murphy Report came as no great surprise. To others, who had been less ready to believe that things were so bad, Judge Murphy made it impossible to evade the truth and its consequences. Their trust had been shattered.

Whatever happens now, there is no turning back. The Catholic Church will survive as a vibrant force in people's lives only if it can faciliate people spiritually and intellectually in ways that are honest, realistic and compelling. This will require new forms and radical thinking, at a time when the number of priests and nuns with deep training in liturgical traditions and liberating theologies is decreasing. It will need the sort of self-confidence and reinvention that John XXIII and his Vatican Council had seemed to herald.

So much that is good lies buried so deep within Catholicism that it is invisible to many people. The Church serves no useful purpose for them, except as a service industry for births, marriages and deaths. It looks set to go in Ireland the way of the Anglican Church in England.

Some hope remains that Catholic churches may yet become venues for spiritual renewal and intellectual stimulation. However, the task of retranslation, reinterpretation and connection to contemporary perceptions is a daunting one, and not just within Ireland. Even the language used in services has little meaning for many people educated to see the world in new ways. Couched in imperial jargon and weighed down by centuries of accretions, what is said and sung can be alienating rather than enlightening in this era saturated by complex information.

The Irish Church itself is encased within a universal structure that has evolved in a manner that seems to militate against necessary change. The failure to debate issues relating to the manner of appointment and accountability of bishops, the gender of priests and the possibility of married priests, is a major barrier to religion ever again reaching people for the first time in a way that is intensely personal or spiritual.

The authorities of the Catholic Church, who control its levers of power and determine its direction, might fruitfully reflect on this question asked by Jesus: 'What father among you, if his son asks for bread, would give him a stone, or if he asks for a fish, would give him a snake instead of the fish?'[6] Apologies for child

6. Luke 11:11 (International Standard Version translation).

sexual abuse, for the snakes let loose on children and their families and communities, are of little value in the long term if authorities cannot grasp that clean water is needed so that fish (an
early symbol of Christ) may swim again in the institutional
pond. Without straining this metaphor, one may add that transparency is often a sign of clean water.

One of the principal reasons why people are falling away
from Catholicism as it presents itself in practice is that they experience it as a stone, as something cold and inert and, unlike
the bread of life, not nourishing. Expecting them to use devotional formulas that no longer have meaning for them and that
are not connected with contemporary scientific and philosophi-
cal views of the world is literally a waste of time. It is as futile as
urging a Greek to climb Mount Olympus in the hope that he will
literally find Zeus there.

And it is vain to think that the Irish Catholic Church will necessarily become more vital as it shrinks, that somehow the institution is simply shedding its lukewarm or insincere adherents.
This view is simultaneously judgemental and self-satisfied. One
may not assume that those who remain are more courageous or
honest spiritually than those who leave. It may be that many
loyal members are simply unthinking or fearful.

The hierarchy could even make matters worse if it now pur-
ports to empower the laity while simply passing limited powers
to a caucus of lay people whose conservatism is as much ideo-
logical as it is theological. Either the Church is everyone or it is
not.

Irish Catholics reflecting on the current woes of their Church
are less disinclined than were their ancestors to think that the
Reformation was reasonable. History has moved on for now, at
least south of the border, and many citizens of a better educated
and wealthier Ireland find paternalism unbearable. They tend to
agree with Protestants on matters such as contraception and
divorce, married and women priests, and greater accountability
in Church governance. However, for some born into the Catholic
tradition, the alienation is even more fundamental: they, like
Matthew Arnold (1822-88) standing on the shore one hundred
and fifty years ago, find that:

The Sea of Faith
Was once, too, at the full, and round earth's shore
Lay like the folds of a bright girdle furl'd.
But now I only hear
Its melancholy, long, withdrawing roar,
Retreating, to the breath
Of the night-wind, down the vast edges drear
And naked shingles of the world.[7]

The gap between the actual place where many Irish now find themselves spiritually and the Catholic Church cannot easily be bridged or closed. Clinging to old forms and old ways is a type of idolatry and, if changes are needed, then a failure of nerve will appear to reflect an absence of faith on the part of Church authorities. Those who really believe in the continuing power of Jesus to influence events and people have no need to defend institutional privileges and practices appropriate to other times or places.

Is it in fact possible for the Catholic Church to persuade men and women that there is a place for them within the Christian community, based on heartfelt conviction, and not on blind faith in dogma or lip-service to liturgies that have outlived their value as an expression of what lies at the heart of Christianity?

There are those who hope that economic and other reversals in the good fortune of Ireland will drive people back into the arms of a mothering Church. It is a miserable way to view religion, to regard it fundamentally as the resort of the despairing and crushed. While Christians should always attempt to help people in need, to console the broken and defeated, those of deep faith do not wish for the suffering of others or need it to justify their existence. Instead, they try to build God's 'kingdom' on earth, which implies a better and happier and fulfilling world. The future welfare of the Irish Catholic Church will depend on those who, like the first apostles, choose freely to be Christians because they find within that Church both truths and spiritual satisfactions.

Religion must enhance the mind. Faith ought to complement science rather than oppose or suppress it. The Sacred Mind is

7. From 'Dover Beach'.

one to which we can aspire, one where no preconditions are set on thinking about the universe and where religion aids further understanding rather than stifling investigation. In this context, the Catholic Church needs to revisit not only its views on matters such as contraception or married priests, but also its understanding of issues such as papal infallibility, or the virgin birth, or transubstantiation. Insofar as these were ever more than obscure, debatable, formulations of concepts with little practical implication for believers, they were surely never meant to constitute an insurmountable barrier to evangelisation. The Sabbath was made for man, not man for the Sabbath.

The Catholic Church must present modern people with an account of creation and its relationship to the divine that is stripped bare of many non-essentials that may have helped to sustain the institution in other eras. To do this requires a great intellectual and artistic undertaking, a reinterpretation of concepts such as saints and angels, a reinvention of language to conform with modern forms of expression and understanding and a rewriting of much of the liturgy to chime with contemporary forms of creative expression and intellectual insight.

This is not a matter of the Church being fashionable or trendy. We have had rather too much of the superficially 'relevant', of a presentational process that has been appropriately lampooned by, for example, the *Father Ted* television series. It is, instead, a matter of the Church being present to a world in which spiritual hunger recurs and cannot be satisfied by simplistic formulas. Does the current training and lifestyle of priests and bishops in Ireland equip them to understand the perceptions and anxieties of their fellow citizens, and enable or free them to address these in a broad and engaging way?

The Sacred Mind recognises the fact that thinking itself can be a form of liberation, and that when it is coupled with the compassionate insights of Jesus and other great teachers it may be a source of joy and an antidote to the oppression of everyday demands and needs.

For its part, the Sacred Heart is aware of the interconnectedness of all sentient beings and all matter. That awareness can be experienced as a warmth and strength that is both physical and emotional. It is an opening to the energy of Jesus through which our bodies may become receivers and transmitters of the white light of love. For this visualisation to be sustained as fruitful spiritual practice, and not simply tend towards occasional or even dangerous emotionalism, it should be cultivated within a wise and structured tradition. It will thus draw strength from centuries of meditative and contemplative experience within world faiths, including Christianity and Buddhism, as well as from the practices of penance (humility) and communion (social responsibility).

However, the minds and hearts of many people in Ireland are no longer being reached by religious organisations. When they visit churches they experience little intellectual or physical connection with the liturgies and prayers. There is no binding back to any point on earth or in the heavens where they sense that they belong. Who could seriously expect most modern Irish people to sing with conviction or enthusiasm many of the hymns trotted out in churches, which were written for people of other eras? This is not to say that some hymns, perhaps especially the oldest and those based on the Psalms, could not take on new life if people learned to appreciate them in new ways with the fresh insights of sacred minds versed in liberating theologies and biblical scholarship and to embrace them with the joy of sacred hearts filled with a new understanding of incarnation. But a great deal of what is set out at present in liturgies is a dead letter, and the quality cannot compete with much of the music and lyrics available on iTunes.

Yet even today *The Sacred Heart Messenger*, that inexpensive and monthly 'little red book' so long found in many Irish homes, is said to have a circulation of 120,000 copies internationally. Its editor believes that this is so because, 'the *Messenger* concentrates on the accessible spirituality of the heart of Jesus, offering nourishment to many people who feel themselves starved of anything to keep their faith alive.'[8]

A new kind of meditative devotion to the symbol of sacred compassion, that burning heart of Jesus, might be a means for people to revive the spark of a religious faith that has everyday

8. John Looby, 'About *Messenger*', at http://www.messenger.ie/ About_ Messenger_.aspx (13/01/10).

meaning. To this end, an understanding of some of the meditative practices and visualisations of Buddhist traditions could be
very helpful and, in this context, dialogues such as that between
the Dalai Lama and Christians have provided a basis on which
to explore further possibilities.[9] Buddhist teaching and practice
invites people to live life in a way that experientially connects
daily existence with their intellectual convictions and with a
broad spiritual outlook.

The image of the Sacred Heart can be an enabling visualisation for compassionate practice by modern Christians, including
those who no longer connect in any deep way with much of the
doctrinal and liturgical verbiage of their Church or former
Church. An image that meant so much to many of our ancestors
is worth a second glance, as one theologian and therapist also
recently argued.[10]

From the seventeenth century, the heart of Jesus came to
have a special fascination for some Christians. This was largely
due to the dedication of a French Catholic nun, Margaret Mary
Alacoque (1647-1690), who 'enjoyed familiar conversations with
Our Lord, who himself directed her spiritual life.'[11] The devotion
was sometimes used to support conservative political object-
ives.[12]

There are aspects of the cult of the Sacred Heart as it developed that may today seem excessively emotional and prescrip-
tive. We may think that the relationship between the individual
devotee and the object of devotion in some cases verged on the
erotic or even psychotic. Was it a subconscious alternative to, or
substitute for, satisfying forms of human relationships that were
unavailable? The devotion was sometimes also predicated upon
expectations of direct material or heavenly returns that seem
unduly self-centred. Moreover, in pious writings about the de-

---

9. See, for example, Dalai Lama, *The Good Heart* (London, 1997), passim.
10. David Richo, *The Sacred Heart of the World: Restoring Mystical
Devotion to our Spiritual Life* (Mahwah, NJ, 2007).
11. Patrick O'Connell, *The Devotion to the Sacred Heart of Jesus: The
Essence of Christianity and the Centre of the Divine Plan of Redemption*
(Wexford, 1951), p 3.
12. Raymond Jonas, *France and the Cult of the Sacred Heart: An Epic Tale
for Modern Times* (Berkeley, CA, 2001), passim.

votion, the ultimate objective often appears to be more about perfecting oneself than about helping others, although perhaps it is fairer to say that the performance of good deeds remained an implicit condition or outcome of the practice.

On the other hand, superficial deconstructions of saintly hagiographies do a disservice to those who lived in pre-Freudian times. The devotional experiences of celibate women such as Teresa of Avila or Margaret Mary Alacoque, and their eloquently energetic descriptions of them, may well mimic, mirror or even sublimate physical yearnings about which we are more frankly open today, but this does not vitiate the underlying value of visualisation in terms of cultivating appropriate motivation and helping us to bear in mind qualities that we admire in others.

Our ancestors venerated the Sacred Heart because the image represented something good and morally empowering. Whatever difficulties they faced by way of material hardship, personal tragedy or political repression, they found a place in their homes to reflect on compassion and motivation. Although Salvador Dalí as *enfant terrible* had traversed his beloved mother's veneration of the Sacred Heart, he subsequently acknowledged another dimension to her devotion by painting in 1962 a version of the image that seems respectful and that may reflect his own complex efforts to reconcile religion, art and science.[13] His version is far less anaemic and more corporeal than some of the pasty prints on sale commercially, while at the same time not being overly muscular in any faux 'manly' way.

At a time when not just the Irish but people generally around the world are facing great climatic and economic uncertainty and experiencing personal alienation, the Sacred Heart could be adopted by new generations as a symbol of their best aspirations and a focus of meditative practice and compassion. However, this will only happen if people are also convinced that religious observations are rooted symbolically in a view of the world that is aesthetically and intellectually defensible in the light of current scientific insights, including those of psychology and sociology.

13. National Gallery of Victoria, 'Dalí and religion', at http://www.ngv.vic.gov.au/dali/salvador/resources/DaliandReligi on.pdf (13/01/10).

The Sacred Mind and Sacred Heart depend on one another. Understood as they have been explained above, they also comprise a vision of faith that transcends the period considered by Judge Murphy, and that can help to redeem an institution severely compromised by the suffering of those who in Dublin or elsewhere survived or did not survive abuse by people who styled themselves religious or spiritual when they were not in fact so in any authentic sense of those words. While even the most conscientious and careful person cannot avoid falling into sin, the sustained levels of abuse of power and abuse of children within the Church might have been lower had popes, cardinals and bishops fostered a greater awareness of what the religious life must and must not entail both physically and spiritually. In that respect, Pope Benedict was quite right to remark, as a statement issued by the Vatican after his meeting with the Irish bishops on 15 and 16 February 2010 records him remarking, that 'the weakening of faith has been a significant contributing factor in the phenomenon of the sexual abuse of minors' and to point to the need for a deeper theological reflection on the whole issue.

Theological reflection will be most frutiful if it can take place within a context in which the demon of child abuse has been exorcised from the institutions of the Catholic Church. That possibility has been made more remote by disagreements within the hierarchy about what course of action some bishops named in Judge Murphy's report on the Dublin Archdiocese should take. This has implications for bishops elsewhere. The consequences of covering up sex abuse in Ireland, Germany, and other countries were terrible for children and have compromised the highest authorities within the Catholic Church at home and abroad. It is difficult to see how an instituion so compromised can embark on significant theological reflection and spiritual renewal without a fundamental reform of the way in which all of its members communicate and do business with each other and with the broader public. Recitations of regret, and new reporting procedures for abuse, are insufficient.

Meanwhile, as the scandal continues to unfold, people who have not lost faith (and even those who have) may gently echo from a litany recited by some of our ancestors the prayer: 'Sacred Heart of Jesus, Son of the Eternal Father, have mercy on us.'

CHAPTER FOUR

Parent AND Bishop

Richard Clarke

The double perspective – as both a parent and a bishop – that I am able to take on the Murphy Report is undoubtedly unusual in the Irish context, and I must admit that it is probably for this reason alone that I believed I might reasonably participate in an exercise such as this. It is certain that no-one will be able to take a measured or detached view of the Murphy Report for quite some time, but there are perhaps some things which may usefully be said or written in an immediate response.

As the parent of a son and a daughter whom I love very much, I find feelings of nausea, rage and loathing truly difficult to suppress when I read in the Report of the perverted treatment of defenceless children at the hands of those who were actually entrusted with their care. My son and daughter may now be adults but, as I have discovered, the protective instincts of a parent at any stage in life do not in fact diminish, and I know full well the vicious ferocity I would most certainly experience even now if I ever learnt that my son or daughter had been intentionally damaged – emotionally, physically or sexually – in their defenceless and innocent years in order to satisfy the corrupt compulsions of an adult to whose care they had been entrusted.

As a bishop of the Church of God, I can only bow my own head in sadness and shame that the gospel itself has been besmirched for so many in Ireland today – men, women and children who can no longer see the face of Jesus Christ *anywhere*, because numbers of his anointed servants have used their position of trust within the Christian community to prey on children and to take their sacred innocence from them. Not one of us who has received the privilege of ordination can claim to have come even remotely close to living up to the calling we have been given by God, but that cannot blind us to the particularity of the destruction of children – those who were so much loved, and treated

with such immense reverence, by Christ himself. A deeply disturbing aspect of these terrible revelations must be that many of
those who have been abused by priests have now lost their faith
in God, because they can associate religion only with mistreatment, perversion and sadism. Certainly there are others – already antagonistic to the Church, but who themselves have not
suffered abuse – who have used the Murphy Report (like the
Ryan Report before it) as justification for the vilification of all
religious faith. But can we say with any certainty that there are
not also many who would wish to believe, but for whom this report has been a final straw that has broken their will to follow
Christ? No Christian disciple of any tradition can feel anything
other than distress if any of their fellow pilgrims will have lost
their tenuous hold on Christian faith through what they have
learnt of the behaviour of some of those who were entrusted
with pastoral care within the Church of God.

But seeking to look with some element of detachment at the
Report, what might we now say for certain that we must carry
into the future? We now know – if we did not know before – the
appalling depths of depravity to which abusers of children are
able to travel, and we know the terrible and unending emotional
damage that any abuse of any kind can do to a child. We now
know also that child abusers are extraordinarily manipulative
individuals, and train themselves relentlessly to be immensely
plausible, and even apparently 'likeable'. We know that human
conscience can be so utterly suppressed that an abuser, when
brought to book, may even cast himself (or herself) as the real
victim of what took place. We know also that a stern lecture and
the offer of 'a fresh start' for an abuser of children is as risible as
gently warning an alcoholic of the dangers of excessive drinking
and then handing him or her a bottle of whiskey as a sign of
trust and friendship. The pathological disorder that leads to child
abuse cannot be removed from the human psyche, least of all by
the individual abuser concerned. It can at best be contained, but
only with the constant vigilance and support of others. We know
that even the most unlikely of people may be abusers, and that a
propensity to abuse will not necessarily show itself in advance
through isometric psychological tests.

Most of us can have no idea as to the motivation of those in

positions of responsibility now being accused with such bitter-
ness of 'covering up' for the abusers of children. My own feeling, for what it is worth (and it is truly said as a parent rather
than as a bishop), is that it was probably naïvety, gullibility and
a total lack of understanding of the appalling nature of child
abuse or of child abusers rather than any cynical or calculated
determination to preserve reputations, even the reputation of
the institution of the Church itself. Of those bishops who have
felt themselves forced to offer resignations in the wake of the
Murphy Report, I know only two, albeit one of these well. I must
in honesty say that I do not believe that either of them would
ever – intentionally and knowingly – have placed the reputation
of any priest before the spiritual, emotional, sexual or physical
safety of any child. They have, however, accepted responsibility
for a culture which could permit, for whatever reason, the de-
praved denial of a good and wholesome childhood for numbers
of young people.

What all of this means is that no-one can ever again take it
upon himself or herself to make a judgement as to whether a
complaint of abuse is reliable. We know that there will in the
future inevitably be some malicious complaints and even some
wholly false allegations, but no complaint may ever again go
uninvestigated by civil authorities. In the handful of such cases
that have crossed my own path, whether as a rector or a bishop,
I now feel some relief that each was already under investigation
by civil authorities before I was informed. Within the Church of
Ireland's code of practice for child protection, *Safeguarding
Trust*, now enforced by synodical law, every parish is required
to have a 'panel' of parishioners (representing both sexes), to
which any complaint of mistreatment of a child is to be made.
When these protocols were being set up initially, over a decade
ago, it was first planned that it would be the responsibility of the
panel to make a judgement on the reliability of a particular complaint. It was very quickly decided that this was unsafe, and that
every complaint must immediately and automatically be reported
to the civil authorities.

The parochial panel is also required to ensure that the facilities in the parish are physically and environmentally safe for
activities involving children, and that in no situation may any

child be left alone with one adult. Confirmation classes and even the traditional Sunday Schools (the latter often held in the precincts of the church buildings) must have more than one adult present, even where there is a group of children. The General Synod of the Church of Ireland has now made it the legal responsibility of each diocese's Diocesan Council (which consists of elected clergy and laity under the chairmanship of the diocesan bishop) to ensure that all parishes are compliant with the *Safeguarding Trust* regulations, which themselves comply rigidly with state law. If I may in this context presume to give advice to another Christian tradition, it would be to ensure that a bishop is not made wholly responsible for the enforcement of child protection protocols in a diocese. An elected group of clergy and laity from within a diocese may be of huge value in ensuring that there are fewer 'unknown unknowns' which might inadvertently allow danger to children in parishes. It is in any case clearly good practice that *all* ministry to children is best undertaken by more than one individual and, ideally, by people of both sexes working in collaboration.

There is, however, another aspect to the determination to safeguard children under our care – and one which must be taken seriously. We are now creating a culture where children are encouraged to believe that every adult is potentially a predator. The result of this is that adults are now fearful of children, lest any affection shown is misconstrued as a precursor to abuse. This is not a wholesome or a healthy scenario. Recently, I was delighted to officiate at the wedding of a young friend, a former parishioner whom I have known since she was five years old. At the reception, she made a bride's speech during which she thanked me for making the journey to the wedding and for honouring a commitment I had made when she was a young teenager, that I would officiate at her wedding should she marry. She then added, 'As many of you know, Richard and I have been very close friends since I was a little girl'. It was lovely to hear her say such a thing with an utter unselfconsciousness, but as she and I have commented to one another since, will such friendships in the future ever be seen by others as innocent, natural and wholesome? In our adult anxiety to protect ourselves, we now hold children at arm's length, both metaphorically and physically, but are we not also starving them of something which is equally necessary for their well-being, normal adult warmth, kindness and concern for them? Future generations may well look back on ours as the time when children were treated with coldness and distance by any adult who was not a member of their own family. Might this not be another form of 'abuse' of children, when we deprive them of natural relationships with the adult world?

The challenge, therefore, for all our traditions is to provide safe places within our Church communities where children and young people can feel not only secure but also welcome and valued, enjoying pursuits that are of real interest to them. At the same time, children must learn to believe that the adult world is not a place of threat, and that adults can take a generous and altruistic interest in them, without there being any ulterior motive. My own experience as a parent is that activities for children and young people within a parish context are of huge value and are for the most part appreciated by all. My experience as a bishop over the past few years is that it is becoming steadily more difficult to persuade adults to take on responsibilities for young people in a voluntary capacity. If adults are to be in fear of being regarded as potential predators, how can they be expected to give of their time to work with youth groups? Who is going to give up the limited time at their disposal if there is not only no appreciation of their efforts but also the constant danger that their commitment to young people may be misconstrued and vilified?

If there is to be any resolution to this challenge, it is that we seek to ensure that adults of different ages and of both genders are encouraged to work with children and young people in a setting that is demonstrably safe in every way. I emphasise the need for women and men to be involved. It was pointed out at a recent diocesan synod in Meath and Kildare that it is becoming increasingly difficult in parishes to persuade men to become involved in Church activities with children. They have a greater fear than have women, that their involvement may be misinterpreted by children and adults alike. But it was pointed out that children need role models outside their family circle that are not exclusively female. Making the Church a good, safe and welcoming place for children and young people cannot be a matter for the clergy alone. It must be a shared task (if it is not already so), where men and women of all ages can join together unself-consciously in parochial activities with children and young people. Nor is this mere abstract piety: a few days before writing this chapter, I attended a lively pantomime performance at a near-by parish, where more than a hundred people were involved in the production, encompassing every age, from seven to seventies (and including a large number of late teens and early twenties, that most problematic of ages for parish involvement). But it is surely of equal importance that even those areas of parish life that we label as exclusively 'spiritual' rather than 'social' should, as a matter of principle as well as practice, be collaborative, involving clergy with parishioners of all ages and both sexes.

There are clearly rocky times ahead for Church and State, as the entire issue of child abuse is, we may only hope, examined with courage and clarity. There are also areas which the people of Ireland may not yet be ready to face, but which they must face, sooner or later. Whereas the abuse of children by those who are given professional access to them (obviously clergy in particular) is particularly loathsome, at some stage we must widen the consideration of the mistreatment of children by adults. As a few brave people have pointed out, more than thirty times as many children are abused by adults who are not clergy as by clergy. Whereas this does not diminish the particularly re-pulsive nature of the clerical abuse of children, it should not close our eyes to what is clearly a serious societal issue. Child abuse is clearly a significant issue in the whole of society, and just as there has long been a wickedly ambivalent attitude to rape and to domestic violence in this country to which far too many of us have turned a blind eye, so we must never allow child abuse to be neatly sectored as a clerical crime alone and ignore its prevalence elsewhere. None of this is to diminish the appalling truths that the Murphy Report has highlighted nor should it shift attention elsewhere as a cynical distraction from the Report itself, but I would certainly wish, as a citizen of the Republic of Ireland (rather than specifically as a parent or a bishop), that we live in a truthful and open society that has no no-go areas for anyone.

A concomitant challenge, when we as a society are ready to move the question of child abuse into a wider arena than the solely clerical, is that we explicitly accept that because in cases of the ill-treatment of children we have moved our perspective (perhaps inevitably, in order to protect vulnerable victims) from a presumption of innocence to a presumption of guilt, we are then ready to take the consequences of such a stance. In other words, when innocence of a crime against a child or children is established (and this is very far from easy to achieve, although we should always be ready to accept the possibility of such being the case), the individual accused is regarded by society as truly and completely innocent.

As time elapses and we are able to view the Murphy Report with greater detachment and objectivity, there are unquestionably more lessons to be learnt. In the meantime, as a parent and a bishop, I can only sincerely thank those who have had the immense courage to speak the unspeakable, and to shine a piercing light on places of dreadful wickedness which many people would wish had remained closed and concealed. Irish society will never be the same again and nor will the Christian Church in Ireland, in any of its traditions. We must together make the Church in its entirety a better place. We must also pray that those who have lost all faith in the Church through the vile behaviour of some called to be ambassadors of Christ, may be enabled somehow to see again the face of Christ himself, who is to be found in every place, no matter how dark and terrible, and who is always and only on the side of the exploited and of those whom others have sought to destroy.

CHAPTER FIVE

Journey To Loss: Living the Murphy Report

Marie Collins

A few days after the publication of the Murphy Report a lady approached me in the supermarket. She took my hands and said: 'You have been talking about this for years, but it is only now I understand, I understand what you have been telling us.' This lady represents many in the country who for years have heard about clerical sex abuse through the media, by reading the testimony of survivors in the Ferns, Cloyne and Ryan Reports. They have heard the Catholic Church leadership's denials, have listened to the shock they expressed at the Reports, as if it was all news to them. Church leaders claiming that they did not understand abuse, they were doing their best, had been on 'a learning curve'. While suggesting through their apologists that the whole issue was a media conspiracy 'by anti-Catholic journalists,' or that many accusations were false, or that victims who spoke out were only looking for revenge or money. At the same time, those in leadership were constantly making statements about how they always put the safety of children first, that the care for victims and their families was a priority and there had never been any cover up.

All the apparent sincerity, shock and reassurances had convinced many Catholics that their Church leaders were being unfairly blamed for the bad apples in their ranks; they had been doing their best to help survivors and to handle this crisis, which was no fault of theirs. Who would believe, who *could* believe that those at the very top in the Catholic Church, those who would see themselves as our moral leaders, would allow known predators, guilty of rape and other horrors against inno-

---

* Note that numbers included in brackets refer to sections in the *Commission of Investigation: Report into the Catholic Archdiocese of Dublin July 2009* (Murphy Report).

cent children, to remain free in positions of trust to carry on the same crimes against even more children?

The Murphy Report has blown all these denials and obfuscation [1.17-1.9] out of the water. It confirmed that those in Catholic Church leadership in Dublin over decades had known they had predatory paedophiles in their parishes, but instead of reporting their crimes to the Gardaí [1.32] moved them from parish to parish with no concern for the children they were putting at risk. They had deliberately misled survivors and their parents using a uniquely Catholic Church means of lying with an easy conscience called mental reservation [58.20]. The Murphy report said clearly what survivors had been saying for years, that the men in leadership roles in the Church knew what they were doing, but cared more for the institution than for the children [1.15].

The smoke blown in the eyes of the laity had cleared; it was now obvious what had been going on. At last the truth was there for all to see and the Church hierarchy had nowhere to hide. The lady in the supermarket now 'got it'. This encounter left me pondering on how long it had taken me to reach that point and then realise that I could no longer be comfortable as a practising member of my Church. I had not lost my faith through my abuse experience. Sexually assaulted as a child by a priest, I had turned all the blame in on myself [58.4]. When I told my abuser what he was doing was wrong, he said he was a priest, that 'he could do no wrong'. I had been taught to respect and look up to my priests; he was revered and deferred to by the adults around me. I was a Catholic child who had just made her confirmation. I believed him – he was a priest and priests didn't lie. If he was not doing wrong then it must be me. I was left full of confusion, misguided guilt and a total loss of self-esteem. This caused enormous damage to my health and my life but I remained a faithful Catholic.

Twenty five years later I revealed my abuse, for the first time, to a doctor. I came to realise through the work of my doctor that I was not responsible for what had happened to me. I decided I must tell the Church authorities in case this man was still in a place of trust with children. I believed they would take the action needed to ensure he would never be able to repeat his actions on other children. I spoke with a priest in my parish whom I had known for some years. He would not allow me to tell him the name of the abusing priest. He did not want to know the name – saying if he 'knew it' he would 'have to do something': he clearly did not feel he needed to do anything. His reason? He said what had happened had probably been my fault and then went on to tell me I was 'forgiven'! This response devastated me. These words pushed me back into a pit of despair. All that guilt which my doctor had worked so hard to erase came rushing back. Did I question for one minute this priest's sincerity? No. Did I believe him when he said he thought it was probably my fault? Yes. He was a priest and I had great respect for him. Did I realise he was following a Church policy – confirmed by him to the Gardaí nineteen years later? [13.12] Of course I didn't. I was thirty eight years old and a good Catholic all my life. I respected my priests.

This priest's words destroyed all the therapeutic work that my doctor had done. I once more closed down and vowed to myself never to talk to anyone again on the subject. I went on suffering the depressions and anxiety states which had been part of my life since the abuse. My abuser was left unfettered in daily contact with the children in his parish, their parents blissfully unaware of the danger their children were in. As the Murphy Report shows [13.14], during this period he was having ten to twelve year-old children in his house, getting them to change their clothes there before taking them swimming, photographing them and making recordings of them. What else he was doing we can only surmise. But the 'don't ask, don't tell' [1.31] policy was more important to my local priest than any concern about what might be happening to his colleague's young charges.

It was ten more years before I was well enough to try once more to report my abuse to the Church. I wrote to the Archbishop and the day came for me to make a detailed report to the Chancellor of the diocese. I was nervous and emotional. Almost at once he told me he had checked the accused priest's file and there had 'never been a complaint' about him before. Did I believe him? Of course I did. He was a senior priest, a Monsignor. By now I was forty eight years old and still a respectful, trusting Catholic. He asked if I was sure I wanted to go forward with my report and warned that it could end up in court, even suggesting that it might be 'too much for me'. I felt he was truly concerned for me. I was very vulnerable and this made me wonder if I was doing the right thing.

It was now thirty five years since I'd been abused. Maybe the priest had only done it that once and regretted it all his life, maybe it would not be fair to him now to bring it all up. If no one else had ever complained the old feeling that somehow it might be my fault rose in me again. Did I know the Archdiocese had not only proof on file that he was an abuser from the era of my youth [13.5], but also that there had been concerns raised about his behaviour with children by members of his parish only two years before? [13.14] No I did not. I had no inkling it was a policy of the diocese [1.35] and of this Chancellor [1.61] to lie to victims reporting abuse by denying previous complaints, when all the while they knew that such complaints existed. Unaware of this, I wrote to the Chancellor the next day to thank him for his kindness and concern for me!

At this time the hospital authorities where the abuse took place, to whom I had also made a report, contacted the Gardaí and they came to interview me. I also saw my doctor and became firm again in my resolution to carry forward what I had started. I still had no doubts at all about my Catholic faith. I found great consolation during this time in my religion.

I experienced a great deal of anxiety and emotional turmoil in the following months. The abusive experiences of my childhood were constantly on my mind and I needed increased medical assistance. The Chancellor waited five months after the priest had admitted my abuse to tell me. When I asked the Chancellor if he had given this information to the Gardaí, he assured me that he had. Later the Gardaí told me this was not true. I had been relieved when the Chancellor told me my abuser had been removed from his parish, but my relief was short-lived. I soon discovered this was also not true. I then discovered the other admitted instances of criminal acts on my abuser's file. I asked if the Gardaí had been given access to the file, and was told that they had. Again, the Gardaí informed me this was not true [13.39]. Who was lying to me? Why was a self-confessed abuser being left in a position of trust with children? If what the

Gardaí said was true, why was the Church not helping them in every way? Could they be protecting a child abuser? Surely not!

I wrote to the Chancellor to ask my abuser what he had done with an indecent photograph he had taken as part of my assault. He wrote that the priest said he had destroyed the photo. I passed this letter to the Gardaí. I was soon on the receiving end of the Chancellor's wrath – he threatened to sue me for this action. I consulted a barrister who confirmed that my actions were legal and correct. At the same time the Gardaí told me the Chancellor was refusing to sign a statement confirming he wrote the letter. When he discovered that I knew this, he made a complaint against the Garda who had told me – he wanted her punished for being honest with me. I was struggling [13.79] to help the Gardaí investigation and the Church was obstructing this process despite knowing the priest was guilty. I could not believe it! Why? I was beyond doubt and confusion. Now I was angry.

My anger and disillusionment grew over the next months. Numerous attempts to get assurance from the Church that this admitted abuser was not in a parish and would never again be in a ministry in contact with children met with equivocation. The archbishop found my queries 'difficult questions' [13.49]. How could an archbishop of my Church, knowing a man was a paedophile, find it difficult to decide if he should be in a position of trust with young children? The Church always found it so easy to have a moral certainty in how I should live my life – what was morally right or wrong was black and white, no grey areas allowed. Did this only apply to little people like me but not to those in higher places?

I discovered the reasons for the archbishop's difficulty when I met with him some months later. This man was 'a priest', the archbishop told me. I could not 'ruin his life'. He was entitled to his 'good name' and his 'reputation'. The archbishop said that he could ignore the procedures set down in the Catholic Church's own child protection document regarding co-operating with Gardaí and removal from ministry, as they had 'no power in canon or civil law' [13.49][57]. I asked if in that case it was morally right to tell the people the Church was following these guidelines to the letter? He answered that he 'had to follow canon law and his legal advice'. Morality, it seemed, did not matter. Nor did it come into the equation when weighing the abusing priest's 'right to his good name' against the safety of children. I could not reconcile the Church I thought I knew all my life with the Church I was now seeing up close.

The priest was eventually convicted of my abuse and of assaulting another child almost twenty years after me. That day the archbishop issued a public statement[1] saying how 'deeply' he felt for the victims and asking for prayers for us as we had 'suffered so much' and were 'deserving of our special concern'. This made me despair of his hypocrisy. What care or concern had this man or his officials shown privately to me in the previous two years? I had been considered a difficult troublemaker [13.34]. He went on to state: 'The diocese has been co-operating with the Gardaí.' This was a lie intended to mislead the faithful people of the Catholic Church and the wider community. This was mental reservation [58.19/58.20] in operation. It was not a lie to these moral leaders – because they had not said – 'the Diocese has been co-operating *fully*'- the word 'fully' being mentally reserved. The fact that the wording used was meant to deceive the public was fine by them.

This was the final straw. I saw in a new light those moral leaders of my Church who all my life I had looked up to, who preached the gospel and whose rules I had always done my best to follow. They were at ease in ignoring all moral values and behaving in a totally unChristian way to protect an institution that was more important to them than the words of Christ. How had I ever looked up to these men, how could I ever have trusted and respected them, how could I ever believe a word they said again?

I could no longer sit at Mass and listen to a representative of this Church telling me how to live my life when those in leadership were quite prepared to believe none of this applied to them. I am sad to lose an important part of my life. My family and I had always been involved in our parish. My son had been an altar boy, my husband a member of the choir and I a member of a number of parish groups. I ask myself if I can ever find my way back. I still have my Christian belief and I pray as I always

1 Press Release, 27 June 1997.

have. I still believe the Catholic Church is the Church which Jesus Christ founded but I believe it has lost touch not only with the people but also with the very basics on which it was founded. The men in leadership, surrounded as they are by like-minded people and living in a world of canon law and arcane tradition, have completely lost touch with the origins of the Church and with the people who – they constantly tell us – *are* the Church.

While working with the Lynott Group on *Our Children Our Church*[2] we were listing personnel in one section when the term 'lay religious' came up. A canon lawyer in the group stated we could under no circumstances use that terminology. We must use 'un-ordained'. 'Lay' was a derogatory term which would be resented by the religious congregations if used, as in times past the lay religious carried out the manual labour in congregations and so were seen as a lower class than the ordained. It was pointed out that this was the twenty-first century! He insisted 'lay' was a derogatory term and could not be used. The most illuminating aspect of this incident was that the majority of the clerical/religious members of the group could not understand why the lay members found this archaic thinking alarming.

The Vatican to date have not approved mandatory passing to the civil authorities of complaints of child abuse against a priest received by the Church authorities in Ireland. Their stated reason: 'the making of a report put the reputation and good name of a priest at risk' [7.13]. This might come as news to many in Ireland who have been constantly reassured by the hierarchy that all complains are immediately reported. If Jesus Christ were among us now would 'good name' and 'reputation' be his priority or the safety of little children?

After the Murphy report the hierarchy in Ireland must realise that they need to earn back trust and respect. There is only one way to do that. A new era of honesty and humility has to begin, and the laity must be part of the renewal. The Vatican must give its *recognitio* to a policy of mandatory reporting and the State has to be allowed free access to all Church records involving the handling of child abuse allegations past and current. There must be an unambiguous commitment from the Vatican and the Irish

2. Catholic Church Child Protection policy document published in 2005.

hierarchy to the Irish people that mental reservation will *never* be used again in any context.

The Irish Bishops' Conference in their statement of 9 December 2009 stated: 'We are shamed by the scale of extent to which child sexual abuse was covered up in the Archdiocese of Dublin and recognise this indicates a culture that was widespread in the Church. The avoidance of scandal, the preservation of the reputations of individuals and of the Church, took precedence over the safety and welfare of children. This should never have happened and must never be allowed to happen again. We humbly ask for forgiveness.' Within weeks, we had the unedifying sight of former Dublin auxiliary bishops backtracking on this and attacking the current archbishop for actually acting in accordance with it! One bishop (Dermot O'Mahoney) even stated that 'the acceptance by media and current diocese policy that a cover-up took place must be challenged.' The leadership must realise that this is the twenty-first century; that they are now dealing with a well-educated population who will listen to the words and compare them with their actions.

The mechanisms to involve the laity as outlined in Vatican II must be put in place. No longer the two worlds – the ordained above, the laity below: we must go forward side by side. Together, let us get back to being the Church Jesus Christ founded. Then, maybe in time, I will find my way home.

CHAPTER SIX

Jesus the Risen Victim:
A Response to the Murphy Report

Patrick McCafferty

I offer this response to the Murphy Report from the perspective of one who, as a survivor of sexual abuse and a priest within the Church, has been publicly challenging the clerical culture which spawned the scandals and cover-up now exposed. I will also highlight that what was wrong in the Dublin Archdiocese, has been evident elsewhere in the Irish Church, as the bishops have now admitted.

1. My Context: Childhood Abuse
I am a priest of the Diocese of Down and Connor and, in my childhood, I was sexually abused by a female babysitter and a local male youth. The abuse was perpetrated when I was aged between four and seven years old. The abusers were not members of the Catholic Church.

My childhood and teenage years were lived out in the shadows of these happenings. I was filled with dread, anxiety, fearfulness and depression. I was aware of a deep sorrow which weighed me down and from which I could not escape. Only in my relationship with God, as a child, did I find comfort and hope. From very early on, I felt called to the priesthood.

When I was nine years old, I overheard my father observing to my mother about me: 'He is carrying all the worries of the world on his wee shoulders.' They, of course, did not know what had happened. Only as an adult, just after my fortieth birthday, was I able to disclose my abuse to my family as, by that stage, I was in the midst of a severe crisis and needed urgent help with the trauma that had haunted me since childhood.

2. Sexual abuse when I was a Seminarian (1983-1986)
As well as telling my family about the abuse in childhood, I also disclosed that I had been sexually abused by a priest of Down

and Connor Diocese, Fr X, during my seminary training. As a seminarian, although no longer a minor in law, I looked very young. I had the build and appearance of a fourteen to fifteen year old boy. My physical development had not finished. I was very slight of frame. Fr X was much stronger than I was physically.

The abuse I suffered at the hands of Fr X had further serious consequences. I was ashamed and deeply distressed. I felt desolate and overwhelmed by what was happening. Within the diocesan and seminary systems, at that time, there was no one to turn to for help and it would have been unthinkable, on account of shame and fear, to tell anyone in authority. I believed if I had reported the incidents, I would be the one in serious trouble and not Fr X.

The seminary in question was St Peter's College, Wexford, which would later feature in the Ferns Report and where notorious offenders had exercised influence. However, it was when I was home from the seminary on vacation, in Belfast, that Fr X would strike.

His predations plunged me into very dark depths. Looking back, undoubtedly, I was clinically depressed and my distress became noticeable to the seminary authorities who brought it to the attention of the Bishop of Down and Connor, the Most Rev Cahal B. Daly. He sent for me during the summer vacation of 1986.

In reaction to Fr X's abuse, I had started going out to discos with friends and dating girls in an attempt to find a 'normal' life. These activities were forbidden to seminarians and I had been informed on. Bishop Daly was severe with me and accused me of being 'immature'. He told me that I was not being allowed to return to the seminary in September and that I was to 'prove to [him] that I was a man and go and find a job'.

My confusion and distress was being caused by Fr X's behaviour, and being 'punished' in this way underlined to me that the abuse was my fault and that I would, indeed, be blamed had I dared disclose what was happening. I had felt called to the priesthood since very early in my childhood. I was devastated that I was being 'kicked out' but all I could do was accept it. I found a job stocking shelves in Marks and Spencer.

I do not want to detract from the memory of the late Cardinal

Cahal Daly in recounting this experience. He was a man of great goodness and holiness. He did not know what I was going through at that time and I couldn't find the courage to tell him or anyone, at that time. I'm sure that he would have been horrified had he known the full story.

3. Maynooth and Ordination (1987-1989)

Unknowingly, Bishop Daly did me a great favour, in September 1987, when he accepted me back as a student for the Diocese of Down and Connor, by sending me to St Patrick's College, Maynooth to resume my studies. In Maynooth, I encountered great friends who would be my mainstay of support throughout the ordeals that lay ahead, as I tried to recover from the legacy of abuse in childhood and Fr X's sexual assaults when I was a young adult.

In Maynooth, I was happy and Fr X lost his grip on me and faded out of my life. Nevertheless, although Fr X was no longer abusing me, there was still the legacy of having been abused in childhood, compounded by his later actions. I had been traumatised already when Fr X entered the scene and he wounded me further.

I was ordained on 25 June 1989 in St Peter's Cathedral, Belfast, by Bishop Cahal Daly. It was a conviction at the core of my existence that God meant me to serve God and God's People, in the Church, as a priest. I have never regretted offering myself for service as a priest. I have never doubted the truth of my vocation. However, I was deeply wounded by my previous experiences and was suffering greatly as a result.

It was more of a private hell than a public one. Thank God, I was able to carry out effectively all the obligations of my ministry. When I was alone, however, I was full of sorrow and pain. There would be weeks of sleeplessness. When sleep did come, it was Technicolor Nightmare world in 3D. I used to dread sleep. I slept in my living room on the settee, for years, because I did not feel safe in a bed.

4. Post-traumatic stress

I was unwell with depression and anxiety. I was on medication to try and alleviate these conditions. I was self-harming with razor blades on my arms. I pummelled my legs with my fists until they were black and blue. I was suffering from bulimia. I was having panic attacks and flashbacks. I was full of such rage that often left me feeling as if an express train had sped through my chest. I had suicidal thoughts and ideation.

My doctor later told me, in calmer times, after I had worked through much of the abuse in counselling, that he was glad that I no longer came in to see him 'like a hunted animal'. The counsellor, with whom I later worked in the USA, diagnosed post-traumatic stress syndrome which, he said, had been present for years.

Despite being able to continue my priestly ministry, there was a huge personal toll on my health and wellbeing. I was ordained around the time of revelations of sexual abuse by clergy first coming into the public domain. Brendan Smyth was one of the first of such high profile cases. Very quickly, I identified with the victims in their suffering and became very outspoken, as a priest, on the Church's poor handling of these crises and non-responsiveness to those affected.

5. Publicly challenging the Church
I began to challenge publicly the institutional Church about its attitude towards abuse by clergy and its treatment of those who had been so profoundly hurt. My first article on the subject was published in The Furrow in 1996 which described abuse of power, out of which had arisen the scandals of child sexual abuse, as 'the Church's unconfessed sin.'[1]

This article was the first of many, calling upon the institutional Church to respond with genuine Christ-like care, with love, justice and compassion, for survivors of clerical sexual abuse. I made appeals such as the following at the beginning of the Jubilee Year, 2000:

> Think of the lives that have been blighted and so deeply scarred. Remember Christ's words: 'See that you do not despise any of these my little ones' (Mt 18:10). The only medicine for this sickness is humility, repentance and reparation.

1. See P. McCafferty, 'Abuse of Power: The Church's Unconfessed Sin', in The Furrow, November 1996, pp 637-639.

If this cure is not urgently sought by the Irish Catholic Church then God's judgement will surely come. He loves the weak and helpless. He hears the victims' cries and scatters the proud-hearted (Lk 1:51).[2]

On 13 December 2002, Cardinal Bernard Law's resignation as Archbishop of Boston was accepted by Pope John Paul II. Law had been heavily criticised for his handling of abuse cases by clergy in the Boston diocese. This, for me, given my appeals for accountability and greater rectitude in the Church's response to the clergy abuse crises, was a defining moment. That evening, a Friday, I wrote a piece for *The Irish News* calling upon all bishops who had mishandled clerical sexual abuse, in Ireland and elsewhere, to follow Law's example and resign.[3]

6. Call for the resignation of Cardinal Desmond Connell
On Sunday evening, 15 December 2002, I was contacted by a journalist from *The Irish News*, who wanted to ask one important question: 'Should Cardinal Connell now resign also?' Cardinal Connell had been found wanting in the wake of an RTÉ *Prime Time* special feature, *Cardinal Secrets*, broadcast on Thursday 17 October.[4] The Cardinal had admitted 'he made mistakes in dealing with complaints of abuse'.[5] I replied that I believed he should resign. It was headline news on Monday 16 December 2002.[6]

All of this happened ten years before the Murphy Report was published on 26 November 2010.[7] We have also had previously the Ferns Report released by the Irish Government on 25 October 2005 and The Commission to Inquire into Child Abuse, known popularly as the Ryan Report, published on 20 May 2009. We have had numerous scandals and incidences of mishandling by persons in positions of responsibility in the Catholic Church.

---

2. *The Irish News*, Letters to the Editor, 6 January 2000.
3. *The Irish News*, 16 December 2002.
4. http://www.rte.ie/news/2002/1017/primetime.html, accessed at 14:30 on 29 January, 2010.
5. http://www.rte.ie/news/2002/1216/abuse01.html, accessed at 15:30 on 29 January 2010.
6. http://www.rte.ie/news/2002/1216/abuse01_av.html, accessed at 15:40 on 29 January 2010.
7. cf http://www.dacoi.ie/ ,accessed at 15:45 on 29 January 2010.

Within the pages of these reports, there is a multitude of human beings whose lives have been devastated by clergy sexual abuse. There are countless others whose stories are not recorded. My reaction to the Murphy Report is influenced and energised by my own experiences of sexual abuse in childhood, when I was in the seminary and my battle, to this day, for survival.

This has been true of my response to the scandals and the public stand I have taken for sixteen years. I spoke out, initially, in fear and trepidation of how the hierarchy might react towards me; but, because I know the pain of survivors, I reached a decision whereby, in conscience, no matter what the consequences, I had to speak out and challenge the sinful nature of the institutional Church's attitude to survivors of abuse by clergy.

My views were not welcomed by most of those with power in the institution. I was viewed as 'a trouble-maker'. There were, for example, letters written to the press under made-up identities and pseudonyms, attacking and attempting to undermine my position through mockery and mischief. It was obvious, from the tenor of these correspondences, that the authors were a few clerics. Alongside this, I received much support from the laity all over Ireland.

7. *The prevailing clerical culture*
In the Murphy Report, Cardinal Connell was the subject of further criticism and four Irish bishops have resigned or offered their resignations since its publication. Bishop Jim Moriarty, who had served as an auxiliary bishop in Dublin (1991-2002), was one of them and, in offering his resignation to Pope Benedict XVI on 24 December 2009, he said:

> I fully accept the overall conclusion of the commission – that the attempts by Church authorities to 'protect the Church' and 'avoid scandal' had the most dreadful consequences for children and were deeply wrong ... I accept that, from the time I became an auxiliary bishop, I should have challenged the prevailing culture.[8]

8. http://www.catholicbishops.ie/media-centre/press-release-archive/ 64-press-release-archive-2009/1658-23-december-2009-statement-by-bishop-jim-moriarty ,accessed 29 January 2010.

The Irish bishops themselves, in a statement responding to the findings of the Murphy Report acknowledged the prevalence of this culture, not just in the Dublin Archdiocese, but throughout the Irish Church. They said:

We are deeply shocked by the scale and depravity of the abuse as described in the Report. We are shamed by the extent to which child sexual abuse was covered up in the Archdiocese of Dublin and *recognise that this indicates a culture that was widespread in the Church.*[9]

This culture, widespread throughout the Church for so long, needs thorough analysis and exposure to the light so that it can be eradicated, so that genuine conversion and change can occur, within the heart of the Church.

8. Narcissism and clericalism
This culture could be described as the seedbed of the scandals and crises that have so devastated the mission of the Church. The behaviours, attitudes and mores that gave rise to this culture are the very antithesis of the Christian way of life and have no place in a Christ-like, gospel-centred and authentic living out of priestly ministry, in the Spirit of Jesus Christ.

Some experts, who have been studying the sexual abuse crisis in the Catholic Church and its fallout, state categorically that 'the clerical culture of the Catholic Church supports enactment of narcissistic personality features by its priests'.[10] One author lists accepted symptoms of narcissism as presented by the American Psychiatric Association in 2000, as having 'infused' the Church's approach to the scandals. Among these are 'grandiosity, an inflated sense of self-importance, interpersonal exploitation of others, the absence of empathy, a defensive structure privileging the use of projection, primitive idealisation

9. http://www.catholicbishops.ie/media-centre/press-release-archive/64-press-release-archive-2009/1638-9-december-2009, accessed 29 January 2010, emphasis added.
10. T. P. Doyle, 'Clericalism and Catholic Clergy Sexual Abuse', in M. G. Frawley-O'Dea, V. Goldner (eds), *Predatory Priests, Silenced Victims: The Sexual Abuse Crisis and the Catholic Church*, (Mahwah, New Jersey, London: The Analytic Press, 2007), pp 11, 154.

and devaluation, and denial – especially of one's own shortcomings, haughty behaviours and attitudes'.[11]

Thus, we can see how the ministerial priesthood, which is intended as a way of being characterised by humble service of God and the People of God, becomes infected and poisoned by selfishness, self-love and self-absorption. The toxic and dysfunctional mannerisms and character of this anti-priesthood have been termed 'clericalism' by many commentators and it has been defined as follows:

> Clericalism is the conscious or unconscious concern to promote the particular interests of the clergy and to protect the privilege and power that traditionally has been conceded to those in the clerical state ... Among its chief manifestations are an authoritarian style of ministerial leadership, a rigidly hierarchical worldview, and a virtual identification of the holiness and grace of the church with the clerical state and thereby with the cleric himself.[12]

Clericalism has been identified as 'a close relative of pathological narcissism'[13] and this cult of self-love and self-adoration builds around itself 'a culture of secrecy and elitism that is conducive to covering up a scandal like the sexual abuse of minors by priests'. [14]

Narcissistic clericalism, therefore, spells inevitable disaster for the very life and essence of the Church. It is an assault from within on the very nature and being of the Church. It is far removed from the mindset envisaged by St Paul: 'Have this mind among yourselves, the mind of Christ Jesus ... Who emptied himself, taking the form of a slave ...' (See Phil 2:1-8).

9. 'The Mystery of Wickedness'
Clericalist narcissism, that negation of the mind of Christ, is a manifestation of that 'mystery of wickedness' also alluded to by St Paul, whereby lawless mortals behave and present them-

---

11. Ibid.
12. See M. G. Frawley-O'Dea, *Perversion of Power: Sexual Abuse in the Catholic Church* (Nashville: Vanderbilt University Press, 2007), p 9, pp 151-157.
13. Ibid.
14. Ibid.

selves 'as if they were God', in the Sanctuary of God (See 2 Thess 2:4-8). The horror that has been uncovered in the Murphy Report, the rapes and sexual assaults of God's children, along with the cover up by cardinals, archbishops, bishops and other officials, their deaf ears, blind eyes and dumb mouths, manifest this 'mystery of iniquity'.

This is illustrated, I believe, by the persistence still, among many bishops in Ireland, of an attitude towards survivors of clerical sexual abuse that can be described as an absence of empathy masked by a pretence of sympathy. In my own experience and as a result of contact with other survivors, mainly in the North of Ireland, there continues to be a grave lack of any real pastoral charity or human care, towards survivors, by too many bishops.

10. 'For the good of the Church'
A further scandal within these scandals is that those engaged in such cover-up believed they were acting 'for the good of the Church'.[15] There is a Latin phrase said to have originated with St Ignatius Loyola: *sentire cum ecclesia*, 'think with the Church'.[16] No doubt some of those Church leaders implicated in the Murphy Report had managed to convince themselves they were acting out of 'love for the Church', that they were 'thinking with the Church'. This is truly incomprehensible.

At best it can perhaps be seen as delusional thinking and, at worst, cunning disingenuousness. It may have been be a mixture of both, to varying degrees, in various persons. Nevertheless, whatever was going on in these mentalities was certainly twisted and, as a result of their actions and inactions, a very grievous blow has been inflicted on the Church, by Church personnel.

Such harmful and destructive attitudes by clerics, influential or otherwise, are not necessarily confined to the past. Common reactions among some clergy to the scandals of recent years, have been self-pity, blaming of victims and blaming the media. Some have 'described allegations as often unfounded and dri

---

15. See the Murphy Report, 1.15, at http://www. inis.gov.ie/ en/JELR/Part%201.pdf/Files/Part%201.pdf accessed on 2 February 2010, at 17:15.

16. cf. http://reform-network.net/?p=2521 accessed 2 February 2010, at 17:20.

ven by a paranoiac conspiracy to destroy the Church, tarnishing all priests with the same brush and obliterating the good works of so many others'.[17]

This mentality will not serve the Church well as we seek to walk the path of healing with so many of our people who have been hurt. There is enormous work to be done in the present to dissolve the culture of clericalism and cleanse the heart of the Church from narcissism. The road towards healing is going to be slow, painful and difficult and must be walked upon carefully, with reverence, patience, gentleness and humility.

11. Holy anger

It is true that I am angry with the 'institutional' Catholic Church. I feel marginalised and betrayed but I don't give up. It is inconceivable that I would walk away from the Church. A person whom I admire is Gary Bergeron from Lowell, Massachusetts, USA, who, along with other brave survivors, confronted Cardinal Law and the Boston diocese. I point to Gary's example.

Gary, who was sexually abused when he was a child by Fr Joseph Birmingham, has written a book about his experiences. He speaks here about his decision to attend the installation of Bishop Sean O'Malley as Archbishop of Boston:

> You could be on the outside of the Church doors and when they are closed, no one inside hears you. Or you could sit inside, in their home, where they have to look at you, and they can't ignore you.[18]

My staying too is partly a refusal to be ignored, to challenge the toxic silence with my voice, to be an advocate for my fellow survivors. I have been written off in the past by some fellow clergy as 'angry'. I am happy to accept their charge for there is an anger that is 'holy' and 'healthy'[19] which can express itself as follows:

> Or we may not grow tired of telling our own truth in a place where it seemed to have no chance of being heard. Or we are

---

17. J. Merry, 'Beyond the Shock Cycle', in The Furrow, January 2010, p 21.
18. G. Bergeron, Don't Call Me a Victim: Faith, Hope & Sexual Abuse in the Catholic Church (Lowell, MA: Arc Angel Publishing, 2005), pp 19, 277.
19. L. Basset, Holy Anger: Jacob, Job, Jesus (London: Continuum, 2007), III, pp 2, 217.

determined to be healed when the experts consider the case incurable. Or, finally, we will demand justice, we will hope to meet Christ, we will desire to know unconditional love … for as long as it takes, for to renounce it would be to betray ourselves. All this has to do with holy anger.[20]

Jesus Christ is with us always. He is with the survivors of abuse and, true to the scriptures, he is on their side 'against the shepherds' (Ezek 34:10). The word of God remains forever (1 Pet 1:25) and, hearing the cries of the Father's abused children, the sisters and brothers of his Son, these temples of the Holy Spirit, the Eternal Word declares: 'My anger burns hot against the shepherds, and I will punish the leaders; for the Lord Almighty cares for his flock' (Zech 10:3).

12. Staying with the Church

I have often been asked in recent years, given what happened to me at the hands of a priest when I was a seminarian, how I could have continued on the path to the priesthood or remained within the Church at all. My answer is simple. Although my relationship with God was clouded by depression and trauma, I never once doubted that God was present with me and would help me. I believe in God despite what happened and I love God and I have hope. I do not believe I would have survived without faith.

I do not regret for a moment persevering towards ordination for priestly service. I love the priesthood and I have been comforted and strengthened, in the darkest of days, by the celebration of Mass each day since I was ordained on 25 June 1989. When I felt that I had virtually no strength left, I believed, during Mass, that I was being sustained and embraced by the love of the One who was not destroyed by trauma, horror and death – Jesus Christ, the risen victim.

If Jesus has not abandoned me, why would I think for a moment of leaving him? I will do what I can, in collaboration with the People of God, to build the Church that is meant to be by God and to be part of the healing, love, compassion and care that remains vital in the lives of many – not least, my fellow survivors.

---

20. Ibid.

CHAPTER SEVEN

The Disgracing of Catholic Monarchism

Sean O'Conaill

Concentrations of power are not divinely mandated or divinely supported.

That seems to me to be the single most important lesson to be drawn from the catastrophe that overtook the Catholic clerical system in Ireland in the period 1992-2010. Far from being a catastrophe for the Catholic Church, this revelation will liberate and reshape all that is best in Catholicism, including Irish Catholicism, during the rest of this century.

As late as January 2010 no Irish Catholic bishop had publicly recognised why it is that the Catholic Church in Ireland has been exposed by two state inquiries as deficient in its care for children: the fact that power in Western secular society is not concentrated but distributed. Media, courts, government all wield considerable power, but none has the absolute power of a monarch. And it was monarchy, and monarchism, that was finally disgraced in Ireland in 2009.

No Catholic bishop has yet acknowledged that the Ryan and Murphy Reports have clearly revealed that concentrations of power corrupt all institutions that adhere to them. This lack of recognition of something that any bright teenager can see means that the Irish Church, and Catholicism generally, lacks credible leadership from its hierarchy at this time, despite the courageous stand taken by Archbishop Martin of Dublin.

It was the French Enlightenment philosopher, the Baron de Montesquieu, who first noticed that human liberty is best protected by a separation rather than a concentration of power. For intellectuals threatened with imprisonment by the vagaries of monarchical absolutism in early eighteenth-century France, England was a haven. The long drawn out seventeenth-century contest between monarchy and parliament had ended in stalemate in England, creating a rough balance of power. Unable to impose religious uniformity, the aristocratic and mercantile establishment in England had even granted a wide liberty to the press.

Very impressed, Montesquieu developed from this insight the principle of the separation of state power – a principle which became the bedrock of the US Constitution of 1787. It was a principle that proved its durability in the lifetime of many of us, enabling the US Congress, supported by the Supreme Court, to force the resignation of the corrupt President Richard Nixon in 1974. Had Nixon been an absolute monarch, or a military dictator, this could not have happened.

It was essentially the same principle that enabled Catholic families harmed by clerical sexual abuse to launch the first civil suits against the Catholic clerical system in the United States in the 1980s, and to provoke the first criminal prosecutions for this crime. And it was the freedom of the press under that system that made sexual abuse a discussable subject by all news media in the West. Ireland's liberation, beginning in the 1990s, was only a matter of time.

Montesquieu's work had, of course, been placed upon the Roman index in 1751. It is therefore deeply scandalous to the Catholic clerical system that the eventual vindication of Irish Catholic children should be partially a fruit of Montesquieu's insight. There is another deeper scandal, however. The historical sequence that had led to the freedoms that Montesquieu had noticed in early eighteenth-century England had begun with the Protestant Reformation of the 1500s. It was also the religious fragmentation that followed the Reformation that had induced the creators of the US constitution to separate Church and State – another key reason that the crime of Catholic clerical sexual abuse could first be uncovered and prosecuted in the United States.

The conclusion is inescapable. The poorest Irish children in the first seven decades of the life of an independent Ireland were severely penalised by a collusion of the Irish State with the monarchical Catholic clerical system – wedded as the latter was to authoritarianism, clericalism and secrecy. The forces unleashed by greater access to international media in the 1960s eventually brought us into the Western intellectual mainstream – subject to the winds of change initiated by both the Reformation

and the Enlightenment. It was no accident that the first prosecutions for clerical sexual abuse in Ireland were brought by the RUC
(Royal Ulster Constabulary). Or that many of the most forceful
Irish journalists who uncovered the Irish scandal had already been
themselves liberated from deference to Irish Catholic clericalism.

It is almost certainly this historical scandal – the origins of the
liberation of Catholic children in forces hostile to monarchical
Catholicism – that prevents the papacy from doing what Bishop
Geoffrey Robinson requested it to do in 2002 – to undertake a
Church-wide investigation of the causes of the clerical child
abuse catastrophe. This failure also is fast eroding the dwin-
dling credibility of the system, and reinforcing the perception of
many ordinary Catholics that most of their current bishops, and
the Pope also, are on an endless learning curve.

It was, after all, the Catholic historian Lord Acton who formulated the axiom of 1887 that every educated person knows by
heart: 'Power tends to corrupt, and absolute power corrupts absolutely.' We are still awaiting a papal letter that will notice this
principle at work in the Church, and in the corruption of bishops. The fact that we are still waiting is proof of that system's
continued denial of what history is revealing to it. So is the fact
that we are still awaiting a letter that will rise to the challenge of
another sentence in that very same passage from Acton's letters:
'There is no worse heresy than the fact that the office sanctifies
the holder of it.'

Here Acton was clearly indicting both Catholic clericalism
and the monarchical principle – the notion that either kings or
clerics are sanctified by the offices they hold. This axiom is of
supreme importance in the context of clerical child sexual abuse,
because part of the abused child's disempowerment was the
contrasting supreme power assumed by the cleric by virtue of
his office. (Was he not another Christ?) And it was essentially
this heresy that prevented one mother in Ferns from suspecting
any danger in a priest sharing a bed with her own daughter.

The same heresy underlay the preference given by bishops in
Ferns, Cloyne and Dublin to clergy over abused children. It un-
derlay also the disgraceful deference shown by officials in the
Department of Education to those who dominated the dreadful
Catholic institutions indicted in the Ryan Report.

This latter connection is most deeply damaging to Catholic clericalism. Defining Catholic loyalty always in terms of deference to clerical authority, it brought us in 2009 to an inescapable conclusion: the roots of the moral cowardice that prevented Irish civil servants from protecting Irish children from the most grotesque abuse in the residential institutions – and from reforming that system – lay in Catholic clerical authoritarianism.

It was therefore deeply troubling for every thoughtful Irish Catholic to hear Pope Benedict XVI enthusiastically echoing in June 2009 the spiritualised rhetoric of the Curé d'Ars when he inaugurated a 'Year for Priests', with the words 'After God the priest is everything!' Yes of course the morale of Catholic priests is a matter for concern at this most difficult time, but could there have been a better year for the pope to say instead: 'After God the child is everything'? How are we now to believe that this pope has ever come close to grasping the powerlessness of a Catholic child at the hands of a clerical sexual predator? Or to grasping the spiritual damage done by that offence – precisely because the child had typically been taught that 'After God the priest is everything'?

Such rhetoric is therefore deeply offensive to the survivors of clerical sexual abuse, and an insuperable barrier to their reconciliation with the Catholic clerical system. Their lives will be long over before the slow learning curve betrayed by such an utterance will have been completed.

This brings us to another reality. many conscientious Irish Catholics now feel an overwhelming obligation of solidarity with the victims of the Catholic clerical system, and deep anger at the clerical system still stuck on its learning curve. They have a consequent deep need to discover a tradition of Catholic conscience that is not the clerical authoritarian one: 'Your conscience ceases to be Catholic if it does not accord with your bishop's.' This 'take' on conscience was always driven by a need for control. Its rationale was, of course, that without strict obedience 'the church' would fall apart and its core teachings be lost. But just look at the state of the Church in Ireland after four decades of authoritarianism following Vatican II. It is as far as it could be from a haven of peace, harmony and unity.

The reason it is in fact a shambles was brought home to me

soon after I had begun to make contact with some of those who had suffered most from clericalism – survivors of abuse and of the ecclesiastical mishandling of abuse. This had led members of VOTF (Voice of the Faithful) in Derry to report our bishop, Seamus Hegarty, to Rome in 2006. The factuality of our report has never once been contested, but nevertheless I was faced one day with the following indignant question from someone who would consider himself the staunchest of Catholics:

'Who told you to do what you are doing?'

It had obviously never occurred to this person that the primary obligation of a Christian, the obligation of love, might ever require him to act decisively on his own initiative – in opposition to a bishop whose policy and practice were in conflict with that obligation. If we reflect for a moment on what might have prevented those Department of Education officials from taking a Christian initiative in relation to the residential institutions, or on what led Gardaí in the Archdiocese of Dublin to turn a blind eye to the criminal activities of abusive clerics, we will be led inexorably to the conclusion that they lived in total dread of the very same question:

'Who told you to do what you are doing?'

The axiom that lies behind the question must run something like this: Catholic identity is to be defined solely in terms of total obedience and deference to Catholic clerical authority. Unquestioning adherence to that axiom is the root source of the disgrace we have all suffered in 2009. If we do not grasp that fact, and abandon that conviction, we will have learned nothing from what is probably the most traumatic, and important, year of our lives.

To help us to abandon that conviction we need only reflect on an event that took place in our own Church. On the 26 October 2007, in Linz, Austria, our Church beatified Franz Jägerstätter. He had been guillotined by the Nazis in 1942 for refusing to serve in the German army on the eastern front. Critically important is the fact that he had taken this decision in opposition to the pleading of his own bishop who, in common with all of the Austrian hierarchy, had welcomed Hitler's annexation of Austria in 1938, and supported Hitler's war.

The conclusion to be drawn is starkly obvious. Although the *magisterium* will insist upon obedience in all eras, and will insist that a properly informed conscience cannot be disobedient, it may end up with no alternative but to honour a Catholic for disobedience in cases where it has itself been morally deficient.

To rescue ourselves from the moral and ecclesiastical cul de sac into which we were led by clerical authoritarianism we need to recognise that the authoritarian take on conscience (which emphasises obedience) has always been counterbalanced by what could be called the 'divine spark' tradition which accords to the individual the dignity of discernment and judgement, both likely consequences of the indwelling of the Holy Spirit of wisdom within the individual. Exponents of this tradition include St Jerome, Meister Eckhart and Cardinal Newman.

The Catholic Catechism itself expresses this richness by its reference to Newman alongside its emphasis upon the role of the *magisterium* in forming conscience. The conscience of the individual is also, in Newman's words, 'the aboriginal Vicar of Christ'.

Let us suppose for a moment that the following fantastical sequence of events had occurred in Ireland in the aftermath of Vatican II:

> Disturbed by the situation in Ireland's residential institutions for children, a small group of civil servants in Ireland's Department of Education discovered one day in 1966 the references in the Vatican II document *Lumen Gentium* to the 'just freedom which belongs to everyone in this earthly city'. After further thought and prayer, and meditation on Cardinal Newman's teachings on conscience, this 'LG37' group decided to conduct a surprise inspection of a sample of the institutions, and then immediately to leak their findings to the media. These caused a sensation and a crisis of Church and State. Popular outrage led to a more thorough study, which broadly vindicated the original findings and led to a thorough reform of the system in the decade that followed.

Given the climate of the time, this would, of course, have been an almost miraculous occurrence – but so was Franz Jagerstatter's exercise of his own Catholic conscience in Austria in 1942. Had this actually happened, would such an 'LG37' group now be vilified as disobedient Irish Catholics who had acted in defiance of the Church's teachings on obedience and conscience? Or would they be regarded as having vindicated their Church when it was in serious danger of being totally disgraced?

The case I am making is the case made by Joe Dunn in 1994 in *No Lions in the Hierarchy* – for the toleration by the *magisterium* of a loyal opposition within the Church. I believe that case has now conclusively been made by the events of 2009 – because we have all been totally disgraced by the absence of that very thing.

Of course there is a need to be concerned that 'the deposit of faith' is not fractured, dissipated and lost. But what 'deposit of faith' was occupying the minds and hearts of all of those who turned a blind eye to the intense suffering of children in Catholic institutions within living memory? Moreover, there is a crucial distinction to be made between core Catholic belief, and the living out of that belief in the real world. It is now clear that the most senior members of the *magisterium* can make appalling mistakes in the practical application of their faith and in the administration of the Church. An overweening concern to maintain a monolithic Church by penalising any kind of dissent has given us the global Irish Catholic catastrophes of this era. The equation of independence of mind with disloyalty is a mistake we must recognise and rectify, with the greatest urgency.

Just now it seems extremely unlikely that the pastoral letter promised by Pope Benedict XVI to Ireland for the spring of 2010 will rise to these challenges. Given the fact that Catholic bishops have protected abusers in at least twenty-five other countries, the confinement of Church reorganisation to Ireland is entirely indefensible and reeks of the old deadly disease of damage limitation. If there is a sweeping change in personnel at the summit of the Irish Church as a result of this pastoral it will then fall to this new generation of Irish bishops to prove it has learned something from the total failure of the Church system we have inherited.

But whatever happens, the exposure of the total moral failure of Catholic ecclesiastical monarchism will not be lost on future generations of intelligent Irish children. They have already established a tradition of waving goodbye to that system in their teens. There is a good case for arguing that the better part of the

Irish Catholic Church has already escaped from that system, and waits only for itself to be reconvened by a papacy that has recovered its intellectual integrity and finally woken up to the moral superiority of distributed power.

Papal Catholicism has no other viable future.

CHAPTER EIGHT

Communicating the Good News and the Bad

Breda O'Brien

Writing about the significance of the Murphy Report for the Irish Catholic Church and Irish society poses one major problem: the sense that the Murphy Report, instead of bringing closure, is merely one chapter in an ongoing story. There are many hurdles still ahead – the final chapters of the Murphy Report, the report on the Diocese of Cloyne, and the results of the HSE Health Service Executive) audit of how well dioceses are conforming to their own guidelines on child protection. There is also the uncomfortable sense that even if the Church is now succeeding in enforcing child protection policies, there are historical skeletons in the cupboard which may come tumbling out at any stage, thus undermining any work that is being done today.

As a media commentator who is also a practising Catholic, it is a frustrating and depressing time. Shocking and appalling as it is to realise that people charged in a special way with care for the 'little ones' could instead abuse and harm them, it is also shocking to realise that the Church prioritised the prevention of scandal over the protection of children. It has implications for the Church in every area. Due to many factors, we may well be on the way to becoming a minority Church, and the scandals have speeded up that process. Much that worked well within the Church, such as Catholic education, is now under attack, again bolstered by the Church's past failures to protect children, even though child protection policies are now in place in all Catholic schools.

The institutional Church is slow to listen and learn. For many years, committed lay people have been urging the Church to do what Christians should do well – confess, offer sincere sorrow and change their behaviour. To which could be added one aspect that might not apply to the average Catholic in the confessional – to communicate far and wide what you have done and plan to do.

None of this is rocket science. Western Union wrote a guide to crisis management twenty five years ago (*When Every Second Counts – Crisis Communication Planning*, 1984). In summary, it states: Gather all the facts, and disseminate them from one information centre. Speak with one voice, consistently, using designated and trained spokespeople who are credible and fully informed. Be accessible to the media. Report your own bad news – don't wait for the media to dig it out. Tell your story quickly, openly and honestly. If you can't discuss something, explain why. Provide evidence for your statements. Update your communications plan regularly.

It may seem facile to be discussing communications and public relations when so many people have been damaged – at least 2,000 children in the Dublin Archdiocese alone, according to Archbishop Martin. It is true, as survivor Andrew Madden says, that the top priority is that we do not have a new genera-tion telling their story of abuse in twenty or thirty years' time. However, in order to achieve that aim, much depends on clear and comprehensive communication. Further, if people have been grievously harmed, the process of healing cannot take place without sincere and humble communication.

If we return to the checklist, the Church has failed on virtually every count. Take 'gather all the facts, and disseminate them from one information centre'. If the ongoing crisis regarding clerical child abuse has revealed anything, it is the dishevelled and incoherent nature of Church structures. Ian Elliott is the chief executive of an independent body, the National Board for Safeguarding Children (NBSC) in the Catholic Church. He came to public attention when he revealed the Cloyne diocese had not adhered properly to child protection guidelines.

In a speech in November 2009, (http://www. safeguarding. ie/news-1/address byianelliottatthekeepingchildrensafeconfer ence) Elliott said, that as a Presbyterian, he had believed the Catholic Church to be one large but single body with an overall head in charge here in Ireland. He discovered that instead, it is not a single body but rather a number of quite separate ones that are linked. There are dioceses, religious congregations, orders, missionary societies, prelatures, and religious institutions. In all, there are one hundred and eighty four parts to the Church in

Ireland and each has its own head. In a very real sense, no one is in charge. It is an extraordinary achievement that the Church managed to get the one hundred and eighty four parts to agree to a single uniform standard for child protection, and to have it monitored by the NBSC, a body independent of all of them, although still funded by them. It is also one of the Church's best kept secrets. It would be interesting to do research to see what percentage of the Irish public would recognise the name, the National Board for Safeguarding Children, if 'In the Catholic Church' were not tagged on? Or be able to say what its role is?

Ian Elliot discovered that formal communication channels are slow, difficult to access and very limited. I would add that there is also a culture of proud independence. It has often been said in recent times that every bishop is a prince in his own diocese, but it could be said that parish priests have a high degree of independence also. As a result, 'gathering all the facts and disseminating them from one information centre' becomes virtually impossible. It is not that the facts are not known within dioceses. It is that the structures do not exist for sharing them, much less communicating them to wider audiences, until forced to do so by some state inquiry or other. One gets the impression that bishops are uncomfortable to an extraordinary degree with the idea of holding another bishop to account. Instead, even the best of them put their heads down, and get on with doing what they can within the boundaries of their own dioceses. This ignores the reality that the Church is seen as one coherent structure even by committed and informed Catholics, not to speak of the media.

The Murphy Report appeared to be seen as the business of the Dublin Archdiocese. It does not seem to have occurred to anyone to formulate a Church-wide response even among bishops, much less among religious orders or pastoral councils. The same disarray was seen among religious orders in the wake of the Ryan Report, who acted as if they had no unified response formulated in advance of its publication. It is unsurprising, because the structures to do so, as far as can be ascertained, do not exist. Instead, there are *ad hoc* responses, or no responses. The Catholic Communications Office in Maynooth has an impossible job. Certainly, it works well and efficiently in publicising an address or initiative by a bishop, but beyond that, it cannot communicate what does not exist – a coherent and well-planned response to events.

In the wake of the Murphy Report, the Pope expressed the hope 'that the present meeting would help to unify the bishops and enable them to speak with one voice in identifying concrete steps aimed at bringing healing to those who had been abused, encouraging a renewal of faith in Christ and restoring the Church's spiritual and moral credibility.' This is far from a call to unite around the 'lowest common denominator'. Real unity will not be possible without a radical change in the way that Church structures do business.

One of the key developments of Vatican II was the emphasis on using the expertise of lay people 'in the world.' The Catholic Church in Ireland desperately needs the expertise of lay people in basic management and administrative structures and, as part of that, in communications and policy making. This does not require either revolution or heresy – it is mandated by the documents of Vatican II. As the *Decree on the Apostolate of the Laity* states: 'Participators in the function of Christ, priest, prophet and king, the laity have an active part of their own in the life and action of the Church. Their action within the Church communities is so necessary that without it the apostolate of the pastors will frequently be unable to obtain its full effect.'

That document was promulgated in 1965 and it is still not a reality. Lay people used to running, and working in businesses look aghast at Church management and communication policies. There can be a lofty assertion that the Church is no mere business, much less a political party, but that has led not to higher standards of practice in people management, communication or administration, but poorer ones. The hierarchy could learn a great deal from best practice in the secular world about how to manage people and how to communicate. In my limited experience, the Church does consult lay people. Quite often, it then proceeds to ignore most of the advice that has been given.

There is a certain disdain in Church circles for what it perceives as 'spin'. Certainly, if spin means massaging the truth, have nothing to do with it. But if 'spin' means presenting the truth of the situation in a coherent, accessible way, what is wrong with that? (Mind you, the Church has a bit of neck to decry spin, given that it seems to have had no problem with the use of 'mental reservation' – how not to tell the full truth without actively telling a lie. For many Catholics, this was a dreadful admission, and one which compounded their sense of shame at what had gone on.) The Church is supposed to have truth as its core – it is one of the ways in which Christ referred to himself: 'I am the way, the truth, and the life'. When the Church is perceived to prioritise secrecy over truth, it is incredibly damaging to the witness of the institution in every area of its ministry. If the Church is not seen to get it right on something as fundamental as child protection, it will not have credibility in any other area.

Look at the other basics of crisis management: 'Speak with one voice, consistently, using designated and trained spokespeople who are credible and fully informed. Be accessible to the media. Report your own bad news – don't wait for the media to dig it out. Tell your story quickly, openly and honestly. If you can't discuss something, explain why. Provide evidence for your statements. Update your communications plan regularly.' It would be nice if the Church even had a communications plan. Most dioceses don't even have full-time communications people, but instead, it is the job of an already overloaded priest, and often it is the bishop's secretary. In reality, some dioceses are so small they probably don't need a full-time person, but dioceses could pool resources. Again, that would appear to be a shocking concept, given that dioceses don't even share best practice when it comes to pastoral initiatives. One diocese can have a superb family ministry, while a few miles away another diocese may not appear to have even heard of the concept. Communication is not only about bad news. Publicising the good that the Church does is also part of ministry.

As for reporting your own bad news, and not waiting for the media to dig it out, would the Church ever have begun to tackle the problem if journalists had not exposed the problem, time and time again? Certainly, the media impose a political model on the Church, of left and right, that does not fit. There is also a deficit of attention paid when the Church is not in trouble. In contrast to education, or even sport, which is reported 'straight' because so many are interested in it, Church matters are often deemed 'not news' by the mainstream media, unless the news is unflattering. There is a perception that the media in Ireland are hostile to an unwarranted degree. However, there is little admission that the Church may have brought much of this hostility upon itself, and continues to feed it through handling media relations ineptly. Decades ago, veteran religious affairs journalist John Cooney referred to secrecy as the 'eleventh commandment and the eighth sacrament of the Church'. After the Murphy Report, Bishop Kirby of Clonfert acknowledged with commendable honesty this culture of secrecy in the Church emanating from Rome. 'The obligation of secrecy, originally promoted for the best of reasons, led to a culture of cover-up. The necessity to involve our own Irish State and report criminal activities was not emphasised.'

The handling of communications regarding the bishops' Rome visit was a case study in itself. It began promisingly enough, with a press conference which tried to dampen down expectations to a realistic level. One meeting with the Pope, no matter how historic, was not going to solve all problems. It went downhill from there. The visual images of bishops in their full regalia might have signalled the seriousness of the event to Church insiders, but to the general public, it looked like theatrics. The media were frustrated by the lack of briefings during the meeting itself, so it filled the gap both with speculation and interviews with survivors of child abuse. No-one was 'minding the shop' at home. Remember those 'designated and trained spokespeople'? While the bishops were in Rome, there appeared to be no-one who would fit that bill, so not unnaturally, the media turned to Church people prominent in the media. There is an old saying: 'Dog bites man – no news. Man bites dog – news.' It is shorthand for saying that the media are much more interested in the unusual and in dissent than in the normal run of events. Leaving aside survivors, with their more than legitimate reasons for distrust of the Church, those interviewed by the media were always going to contain a disproportionate number of people critical of the Church for a whole variety of reasons. The Church has only itself to blame for that reality, given that it apparently had no-one in place to respond to the Vatican's press statement here at home in Ireland. By the time Archbishop

Martin did a credible job of explaining the statement a day later, the visit had already been framed as a disaster.

There is a further complication. It is extraordinarily difficult to say anything that has the potential to cause pain to survivors. This was illustrated by an incident on the *Today with Pat Kenny* radio show. Veteran Vatican watcher Gerard O'Connell, commenting on the Pope's statement after the visit of the bishops to Rome (*Today with Pat Kenny*, 17 February 2010) suggested that this Pope now had a zero tolerance policy, but that it was some time before the Vatican realised the extent of the problem. A survivor, Michael O'Brien, interjected: 'Please don't say that, because you are hurting me, and hurting me very bad.' Gerard O'Connell persisted, but many others would not. It is a very delicate area, because after decades of not listening to survivors, there is an obvious desire not to add to pain. However, this has led to a situation where to question even the smallest assertion by a survivor is to be open to an allegation to being an apologist for child abuse. This is not healthy. We have seen where putting bishops in a position where they could not be questioned led to. While victims do not have anything approaching the influence or authority of bishops in their heyday, it does not mean that victims are always automatically right in their interpretation of events. Sometimes (like all of us) they will be wrong. These comments should not be in any way construed as denigrating victims. Listening to victims is a key part of any positive future the Church might have.

Dr Monica Applewhite, an American sexual abuse expert, has spent sixteen years assisting organisations to develop best practice standards. Since beginning to work with religious organisations, she has been involved in the development of four US national programmes: two for the Catholic Church, one for the Episcopal Church, and one for the Salvation Army. Speaking in Ireland in November 2009, she recommended that the Church:

1. Provide sexual abuse prevention education that includes, but is not limited to, prevention of sexual abuse by clergy.
2. Establish an advisory council of persons who have been harmed by clerical sexual abuse that includes victims and the families of victims who care for supporting the future of the

Church. Video-tape interviews with them for leaders within the Church to understand their perspectives and hear their voices.

3. Host and participate in a National Day of Prayer for the healing of all victims of sexual abuse.

4. Speak publicly and robustly about your efforts, your commitments, and your beliefs. The faithful are waiting to hear from you.

5. Develop guidelines for which all dioceses and religious institutes will be held accountable.

6. Assist dioceses and religious institutes in the implementation of the strategies.

7. Implement a system of accountability – either audits on an annual basis or accreditation as dioceses and religious institutes become ready.

While the Church has done a good deal on 1, 5, 6, and 7, much of the effort is wasted because of a failure to speak 'publicly and robustly' about these efforts. It is important to realise that the media are not the only audience. Many of the bishops, although not all, issued statements to be read at Masses in their dioceses on the Sunday after the Rome visit. There are not enough of these relatively informal missives. The Catholics in the pews want to hear from their leadership. Perhaps the three 'C's advocated by American crisis management expert, Jonathan Bernstein, apply here: compassionate, competent, confident. There may be a particular application of the three 'C's not envisaged by Mr Bernstein that is relevant to the Catholic Church: compassionate towards victims and their families; competent in handling the crisis and showing that there are structures in place to prevent as far as possible this dreadful evil; and confident, not in themselves, but that the grace of God can lead us to a better place.

CHAPTER NINE

'The boat had moved': The Catholic Church, Conflations and the Need for Critique

Eugene O'Brien

A man from the state of Chu was crossing a river. When the ferry got to the middle of the river, his sword fell into the water. Immediately he took out a knife from his pocket and made a mark on the boat. 'This is where my sword fell off,' he murmured and stepped aside, much relieved. The ferry sailed on and soon got to the dock on the opposite bank. As soon as the boat anchored, the man jumped into the water to look for his sword at the place where he had marked the boat. The boat had moved but the sword had not. Is this not a very foolish way to look for a sword?[1]

To say we are horrified by the recent revelations of child abuse, and of the institutional complicity which sought to avoid the consequences of this abuse in the public domain, is in many ways as effective an exercise as the man from Chu's futile attempt to find his sword by marking the place on the boat where it fell overboard. The abuse of children in a sexual context is heinous, no matter what way you look on it. To be branded a paedophile is probably the worst label that can be bestowed on any adult. Indeed, even in prisons, the harshest treatment meted out by convicts to other convicts is reserved for paedophiles. Some of the details of abuse are just unspeakable; it is appalling to read that 'more than 90% of all witnesses reported being physically abused while in out-of-home care'; it is appalling to read that witnesses to the Ryan Report reported that:

> In addition to being hit and beaten witnesses described other forms of abuse such as being flogged, kicked and otherwise physically assaulted, scalded, burned and held under water.

---

1. *The Annals of Lü Buwei*, trs John Knoblock and Jeffrey Riegel (California: Stanford University Press, 2000), p 371.

Witnesses reported being beaten publicly in front of other staff, residents, patients and pupils as well as in private. Many reports were heard of witnesses being beaten naked and partially clothed, both in private and in front of others. They reported being beaten and physically assaulted with implements that were for the specific purpose of inflicting pain and punishment, such as leather straps, bamboo canes and wooden sticks.[2]

These instances are shocking, but it is the reaction of the Church as a structure which is even more troubling. When the role of an organisation is supposedly the preaching of doctrine and morality to its members, the fact that this organisation then systematically proceeded to deny the abuse perpetrated by some of its members, to obstruct any investigations into the abuse and to protect its own members to the detriment of the victims, often children placed in their trust, is an abomination. To be aware of these crimes and to collude in the avoidance of bringing those responsible to justice, and worse, to redeploy the abusers so that they could abuse again, is an act of criminal conspiracy. And the Murphy report spells this out very clearly:

> Many of the auxiliary bishops also knew of the fact of abuse as did officials such as Monsignor Gerard Sheehy and Monsignor Alex Stenson who worked in the Chancellery. Bishop James Kavanagh, Bishop Dermot O'Mahony, Bishop Laurence Forristal, Bishop Donal Murray and Bishop Brendan Comiskey were aware for many years of complaints and/or suspicions of clerical child sexual abuse in the Archdiocese. (Murphy Report, Part 1, p 6)

In this chapter, I will make no attempt to talk about the individual effects of abuse, as there are others in this book who can speak from personal experience on that issue. It is necessary that we remember what happened so that it can never happen again, but the past is not my concern here; rather, I want to focus on the present and the future of Irish society and on how that society should best react to the structures of the Catholic Church. For me, the core issue is not how the Church responds to the crisis

2. *Commission to Inquire into Child Abuse Report*, Volume 3, p 393.

but how we, as a society, respond to the Church. The Church-
State relationship in Ireland has been categorised by conflations
of perception and knowledge that have blocked serious efforts
to analyse the best course of action that should occur in the wake
of these reports. These conflations parallel the error of marking
the place in the boat where the sword fell out, and they have a
similar effect on the process of finding that sword.

The first conflation is that of 'Irish and Catholic'. Since John
A Costello, leader of the inter-party government, declared: 'I am
an Irishman second; I am a Catholic first',[3] there has been a hand
in glove relationship between the Irish State and the Catholic
Church. This has crossed over party lines, with the hierarchy
given the right of specialised input into aspects of de Valera's
constitution, and with undue and continuing influence on
health and educational matters. The Church, as a partner of the
State, has been almost a given in our culture, to such an extent
that the symbolic power exercised by the Church can blind us to
the actual deeds and behaviour of that Church. This point can
best be clarified in the light of Pierre Bourdieu's discussion of
'symbolic power' and social change. 'To change the world',
Bourdieu argues, 'one has to change the ways of world making,
that is, the vision of the world and the practical operations by
which groups are produced and reproduced.'[4] To date, in Irish
society the Church has to a large extent exercised a monopolistic
symbolic power in that it is central to educational and health
practices and discourses in Irish society. The Catholic Church
exercises *de facto* control over most educational institutions in
the country and in a lot of the health facilities, and these cases of
systemic abuse have given rise to some questioning of the suitability of the Church for such a role. People have talked about
the need for reform within the Church, and of the need for the
Church to heal itself, but this is as misguided as the man from
Chu's efforts to find his sword: it is to look in the wrong place.
The core issue, I would maintain, is not about the Church, but
about secular, civic society (we are a republic after all, at least in

3. Dermot Keogh, *Twentieth Century Ireland: Nation and State* (Dublin:
Gill and Macmillan, 1994), p 208.
4. Pierre Bourdieu, *In Other Words: Essays towards a Reflexive Sociology*
(Stanford: Stanford University Press, 1990), p 137.

name) and how that society should deal with an organisation whose upper management strata in both dioceses and religious orders has been criminally conspiratorial about hiding the crimes of their members. And we are not talking about the long forgotten past here. The Murphy Report spells out the time-span of these complaints very clearly:

> All the archbishops and many of the auxiliary bishops in the period covered by the Commission handled child sexual abuse complaints badly. During the period under review, there were four archbishops – Archbishops McQuaid, Ryan, McNamara and Connell. Not one of them reported his knowledge of child sexual abuse to the Gardaí throughout the 1960s, 1970s, or 1980s. It was not until November 1995 that Archbishop Connell allowed the names of 17 priests about whom the archdiocese had received complaints to be given to the Gardaí. This figure was not complete. At that time there was knowledge within the archdiocese of at least 28 priests against whom there had been complaints. (Murphy Report, Part 1, p 10)

Even as late as February 2010, a paedophile priest, Patrick Hughes, pleaded guilty at Dublin Circuit Criminal Court to four counts of indecent assault against the child, who was then aged between eleven and fourteen, between 1979 and 1983. Detective Sergeant Joseph McLoughlin, who apprehended the priest, agreed that Gardaí were 'getting the run-around from Church authorities'. He said they were initially unable to locate the ac-cused man through the Archbishop's House but a 'liaison priest' contacted him in 2003 and said the accused wished to speak to Gardaí, but the detective then received a call to say the accused would not be attending. That was the last he heard about his lo-cation and efforts to find him were unsuccessful until Gardaí re-ceived a tip-off and Detective Sergeant McLoughlin located the priest in England.[5]

'Getting the run-around' from Church authorities is the issue we need to look at, and it is in this context that we arrive at the second conflation to which I referred earlier. It is all too easy for

5. Fiona Ferguson and Sonya McLean, 'Jailed paedophile priest: it was an altar boy thing', in *Irish Independent*, Wednesday 3 February 2010.

the Church to see itself as moral and ethical in structure, and as far removed from the civil and legal rules and regulations of civic society. At present, there is a strong conflation of the sacred and the secular at play in the way the Church is responding to the different reports. It is as if because the message of the Church is ethical and moral, then *ipso facto* their behaviour must also be seen as ethical and moral and any abuse is just an aberration which can be glossed over by the Church's overall message. To paraphrase Marshall McLuhan, in this case the medium is not the message. As a way of moving forward post the Murphy Report, Irish civil society needs to differentiate between these two modes of knowledge as embodied in the Church and act accordingly.

To claim that the Catholic Church is ethically-driven and that it preaches the gospel of Christ is a way of insulating it from the cause and effect modality of the civil legal system. The key here should not be whether or not the Church does this, but rather how the Church is treated as an organisation within our culture. What the Church claims as its message and *raison d'être* is a matter for itself, but its corporate and systemic actions, enacted in the socio-cultural sphere, should be treated in precisely the same manner as the actions of any other corporate system and organisation. In other words, to preach, for example, about the Sermon on the Mount on a Sunday should in no way protect or absolve those who give our legal system 'the run around' on a Monday.

Rather than seeing the Church as a special case, based on its own claims to a transcendent knowledge and perspective, I would submit that the correct and ethical legacy of the Murphy Report, and that of the Ryan and Ferns Reports, should be that we look at the Church as a temporal and historically-contingent organisation and subject it to the same scrutiny as any other institution in society. Minister Dermot Aherne made the point that 'the bottom line is this: a collar will protect no criminal,'[6] but we have seen few priests and religious sent to jail, and there have been no prosecutions of people in the hierarchy for withholding evidence, or protecting priests, or moving them on to abuse in

---

6. *The Irish Times*, 27 November 2009.

other dioceses when their abuse has been brought to light. Also, the rather supine response of the Taoiseach to the non-compliance of the Papal Nuncio was an indication of the blurring of the roles of the Church in terms of symbolic power:

> The Commission wrote to the Papal Nuncio in February 2007 requesting that he forward to the Commission all documents in his possession relevant to the Commission's terms of reference, *which documents have not already been produced or will not be produced by Archbishop Martin'*. The letter further requested the Papal Nuncio, if he had no such documentation, to confirm this. No reply was received. (Murphy Report, Vol 1, p 37. Original emphasis.)

The Commission again wrote to the Papal Nuncio in 2009 enclosing extracts from the draft report which referred to him and his office as it was required to do. Again, no reply was received. The excuse given by Papal Nuncio Archbishop Giuseppe Leanza, was that the Commission had not gone through the correct diplomatic channels. The Taoiseach said it was 'regrettable' that the Vatican invocation of diplomatic privilege had given 'the impression that the Holy See was refusing to co-operate with the commission', adding: 'The commission and the Holy See, it appears, acted in good faith in this matter, even if the best outcome was not achieved'.[7] Here we see a conflation of the two conflations of which I speak: Cowen, like Costello and de Valera before him, is a Catholic first, as he makes excuses for a lamentable lack of response by the Nuncio, and he has confused the behaviour of the Church as a self-protective secular organisation with the message it preaches. Here it would seem a Roman collar still does provide some protection, and also that there is, in the Taoiseach's mind at least, a blurring between the two forms of knowledge of the Church.

The Church, as spiritual and moral entity, would be expected not alone to comply with the request of a body investigating abuse by its members, but to embrace the chance to undo a wrong. However, the Church as organisation clearly decided to hide behind the dual relationship it has with other countries and

7. www.breakingnews.ie/ireland/eymhgbojsnau/rss2/

invoke the diplomatic letter of the law. Rather than seeing their role as pastoral, the Nuncio chose to see the matter in terms of one country's diplomatic dealings with another. Here we see Bourdieu's symbolic power at work, but here too is the lever with which that power can be deconstructed. If the Catholic Church sees its relationship with Ireland as that of a foreign country, then we, in Ireland, must ask why we allow people whose allegiance seems to be to the Vatican as a foreign state, access to our health and education systems? Would we allow similar latitude to people in an organisation whose first loyalty was to the Queen of Great Britain? Saying that they have a pastoral duty of care is one thing; not responding to a legally instituted inquiry is a more formal example of the State, and its institutions, being given the run-around, albeit at a different level, by the Church authorities yet again. That the Taoiseach is unwilling to call this act what it was – obfuscation of the work of the Commission – is a shame and another example of how the symbolic power of the Church needs to be unpacked and deconstructed if our society is to retain a sense of its own integrity. I am not saying that the Church should no longer be involved in the education of the young in Ireland. What I am saying is that this involvement has generally been taken as a given, without any great sense of questioning as to its validity or utility in the twenty-first century. We need to critique why the State pays for the facilities and the teaching and yet the Church has a presence on 95% of all first, second and third level institutions in Ireland. Given the obfuscatory behaviour of the Church as an organisation in the area of the protection of children, do we want that particular institution so intimately involved with our children? It is a debate that needs to take place.

And this is the crucial point at issue here. Any organisation will close ranks to protect its own members – we have seen it in the financial sector, in politics and in business. Modern organisation theory makes the point about the closed systems of large organisations, which are deemed to be immune to disturbances from outside of the organisation itself, and about centralised and hierarchical modes of power and knowledge, and about the need to protect the organisation at all costs. This means that response to outside factors is invariably defensive and reactive.

There is even an acronym to describe this attitude to maintaining the *status quo* – 'TINA (there is no alternative)'.[8] So rather than judging the Church as a special case, above and beyond the socio-cultural norm, in its own terms *sub specie aeternitatis*, we need to critique it as an immanent and historical structure. We have heard the TINA argument in relation to recapitalising the banks, and in terms of the Church's role in education (who would take their place?), but this is an argument based on a similar premise to that of the marking on the boat. One of the reasons that the Church became involved in education, apart from the obvious one of transmitting their ideology to coming generations, was the scarcity of educated people who could sit on boards of management and run educational institutions. But that no longer applies and there are many people who could now run schools, both primary and secondary, as well as our third level colleges.

This process of critique and debate will have consequences for the interaction of civil society with the Church, and with the mode of knowledge produced by the Church. So, for example, the pronouncements of the Church with respect to women, and women's bodies, and contraception and sexual activity have been seen as a transcendental preoccupation with the value of life. However, if looked at as an immanent structure, then the point could be made that an organisation that is made up of largely middle class, middle aged celibate men would have a very specific viewpoint on issues of sexual activity and on women in general. When such a body makes the point that women cannot be ordained because Christ ordained no women, we can see this as a transcendent form of knowledge or we can wonder why this is the only aspect of the real life of Christ that has been maintained as an exclusionary precept. After all, Christ was a simple Jewish carpenter, but the Catholic Church has not made any of these characteristics a precondition for ordination to the priesthood. Again, looking at the historical and contingent composition of the people making this decision, there would seem to be other reasons to explain the exclusion of women from the ministry. Christ had little truck with the legali-

---

8. Stewart R Clegg, *Modern Organizations: Organization Studies in the Postmodern World* (London: Sage Publications, 1997), p 58.

ties of the Pharisees or with the materialism of the Temple –
how many of the practices of the mitred prelates of our hierarchy could stand up to a scrutiny from this perspective? How
would the man who asked little children to come unto him react
to Archbishop Leanza's prevarication? Or how would he react
to the Taoiseach's defence of this prevarication? Or how would
he react to the hierarchy's hiding behind legal arguments and issues of mental reservation to give the State authorities the 'run
around'? These are all questions that need to be asked by the
people, and answered by the Church.

It is not my purpose here to brand all of the members of the
Church as evil or wrong. I merely want to call to account an
organisation which nimbly switches between a spiritual and
pastoral role and a legalistic and protectionist one. This is
nowhere more sharply illustrated than in two accounts of the
Papal visit to Ireland in 1979. The Pope's visit was often seen as
the highpoint of Catholic hegemony in Ireland. His visits to
Dublin, the youth Mass at Galway and a huge open-air Mass in
Limerick attracted huge crowds and his iconic kissing of the
ground, and his cry of 'young people of Ireland, I love you'
seemed to herald a leader in touch with his people. However, in
St Joseph's Industrial School in Ferryhouse, Clonmel, two boys
were kept back in school and not allowed to go to Limerick to
see him and when the rest of the school had gone, a boy told the
committee that when the rest of the boys left, 'this Brother came
and raped me in my bed' (CICA Investigation Committee
Report (Ryan Report), Vol II, p 87).

The savage irony of this rape taking place while the Pope, the
representative of the Catholic Church, was telling the young
people of Ireland how much he loved them is too bitter for
words. But like all irony, it is instructive: the behaviour of the
Pope with respect to the young people of Ireland was the transcendental face of the Church. The behaviour of the raping
brother, and its subsequent cover up, was that of an organisation which seeks to minimise the effect of wrongdoing.

Similarly, the pomposity of a letter sent by the Interdiocesan
Case Management Advisory Committee, representing the dio-
cese of Cloyne, in response to the proposed publication of the
Cloyne Report captures the mindset I am talking about:

The Church, and its essential pastoral role, is not an optional participant in society but an integral part thereof as designed and mandated by almighty God. Far from being in conflict with each other, the roles of the Church and the statutory agencies of the State are complementary.[9]

Here again, we see the run-around that results in this conflation of power and knowledge and of Church and State. Almighty God is invoked without any question as to how a divine entity would react to his messengers on earth hiding material from an enquiry. The sense is that as representatives of God, the diocese of Cloyne need not be answerable to the State. One might ask how the invoked deity might respond to the results of the Cloyne inquiry which stated that:

However, what are glaringly absent are any references to the need to protect vulnerable young people and to act in a timely and effective way to achieve this end. This is illustrated by the minutes of the Case Management Committee that met on 21 September 2005 to discuss the A case. Current risk to young people is not referred to at all. The suggestion is noted that the option of retirement to the accused might be offered if appropriate. (This is, in fact, what happened when the bishop met the accused later in the month, when he decided to offer to retire from his post.)[10]

One would think that an organisation found guilty of such a lapse in standards would at least mimic contrition and not invoke legal threats about the nature of the Report, but again there is that conflation of the medium and the message to be seen in the letter which states that that:

Your report seriously wrongs the Diocese of Cloyne and our committee. Therefore, if you issue this report in its present

9. *The Irish Times*, 6 January 2009. This is the full text of a letter from the Chairman of the Interdiocesan Case Management Advisory Committee, representing the diocese of Cloyne, to Aidan Canavan, chairman of the National Board for Safeguarding Children (NBSC).
10. Report on the Management of Two Child Protection Cases in the Diocese of Cloyne http://www.cloynediocese.ie/ Bishop%20 on%20 Management%20of%20cases%20NBSC%20report.htm

form or include its distortions in your forthcoming annual report, we shall have no choice but to seek remedies in either ecclesiastical or secular courts or both.[11]

Again, there is no mention of the wrong that clerical abusers do to their victims. The Report was issued, and drew the necessary conclusion that the child protection practice of the diocese of Cloyne 'was significantly deficient in a number of respects', most notably in its failure to 'focus on the needs of the vulnerable child and the requirement to take preventative actions quickly and effectively to secure their wellbeing'.[12] Here, the recourse to legal threats did not result in the 'run-around'. Here the organisation was called to account and the important point to note is that while the organisation huffed and puffed, the Report was published.

On 11 December 2009, in the wake of the publication of the Murphy Report, a statement from the Vatican spoke of the Holy Father being 'deeply disturbed and distressed by its contents'. It described the Pope's profound regret at the actions of some members of the clergy who have betrayed their solemn promises to God, and added that the Church 'will continue to follow this grave matter with the closest attention in order to understand better how these shameful events came to pass and how best to develop effective and secure strategies to prevent any recurrence'. Finally, the statement noted that:

> The Holy Father intends to address a Pastoral Letter to the faithful of Ireland in which he will clearly indicate the initiatives that are to be taken in response to the situation. Finally, His Holiness encourages all those who have dedicated their lives in generous service to children to persevere in their good works in imitation of Christ the Good Shepherd.[13]

11. *The Irish Times*, 6 January 2009.
12. Report on the Management of Two Child Protection Cases in the Diocese of Cloyne http://www.cloynediocese.ie/Bishop%20on%20Management%20of%20cases%20NBSC%20report.htm
13. Vatican Statement after meeting with Irish bishops; *Comunicato: incontro del santo padre con rappresentanti della conferenza episcopale Irlandese e capi dicastero della curia Romana*, http://www.reuters.com/article/idUSTRE5BA1LJ20091211

Again we have the conflation of the act with the message –
Christ indeed was a good shepherd but the Church as an organisation has been very much the opposite. Remember that the
good shepherd in the parable went in search of one of the sheep
that was lost. In the Archdiocese of Dublin, and in Cloyne, the
focus was less on the sheep and more on the shepherd. On learning of the problems of abuse, Archbishop McNamara took out
insurance, which was a sign that he had an eye more to protect
the shepherd than the sheep. And in Cloyne, the HSE (Health
Service Executive) report refers once more to an ongoing lack of
sharing of information with the authorities.

To take the conflations of which I have spoken as givens and
as natural, and to hope that we can progress as a society, is to
demonstrate the same *modus operandi* as the man from Chiu. The
boat has moved and we, as a society, as a republic, must recognise this and dive into the cold waters of critique if we are to
have any hope of finding that metaphorical sword. This is the
task which we must undertake and this is the only way that we
can become a republic in nature as well as in name. I will con-
clude with a classic sample of this in the Irish public sphere. On
Tuesday 26 April 2009, the co ordinator of CORI, Sister Marianne
O'Connor, was interviewed on the breakfast show of Newstalk
FM, by Ivan Yates and Claire Byrne. Yates asked questions
about the property portfolios of the congregations and about the
symbolic tokenism of putting on of extra help-lines in the wake
of the Murphy Report. Then Byrne posed the following question:

> I am just wondering how you would see Jesus Christ react-
> ing today, if he was walking the earth today, how would he
> deal with this, and would he deal with it the way you're deal-
> ing with it this morning?

Sr Marianne replied: 'I don't know how to answer that really.'
That is because such a question unpacks the conflation between
the two types of knowledge structure that we have seen – that of
the moral message and the self-protective system. The boat is
moving and we need to ensure that this motion, powered by
critique and questioning, is ongoing.

CHAPTER TEN

Responding to Abuse: Culture, Leadership and Change

Seán Ruth

Introduction

In the aftermath of the Murphy Report, the credibility of the Roman Catholic Church has hit a new low. Serious questions have been raised about the honesty and integrity of those charged with responding to allegations of clerical child sexual abuse. Questions have also been raised about the culture of an institution that permitted and even facilitated abuse to take place on the scale we have seen reported. The response of the hierarchy has been seen variously as grudging, belated, criminal, unChristian, uncharitable, out of touch and insincere. At the same time, bishops will point to the many occasions when they have apologised for what took place, their calls for renewal in the Church, their efforts to engage with victims of abuse and their commitment to putting procedures in place to ensure the maximum protection for young people in future. It is clear that genuine expressions of sorrow and regret, the acceptance of responsibility for the abuse, inaction and cover-ups that took place, support and reparation for those who were abused, coupled with real commitment to implementing robust child protection processes are basic and essential steps.

While doing right by those who were abused and ensuring it never happens again is fundamental, focusing solely on these is actually not enough to address those factors that allowed abuse to take place on such a wide scale and contributed to the largely inadequate response of the hierarchy. Restoring the credibility of the institution requires more than addressing the issue of child abuse. For this, we need to look at both the leadership and the culture of the Church. In this chapter, I want to examine particular aspects of the leadership and the culture of the Church and how these might need to change in order to restore credibility to the institution, promote a radical renewal and ensure that abuses of any kind will be challenged effectively.

Dysfunctional decision making
The psychologist Irving Janis was fascinated by the ways in which groups that were comprised of otherwise intelligent, well-meaning and moral individuals could make decisions that turned out to be unintelligent, immoral, cruel or dangerous. He coined the term *groupthink* to describe the conditions under which this happened and noted a range of symptoms of this process (Janis, 1972). Among these he included the following: the *illusion of invulnerability* that makes people ignore obvious dangers and be willing to take risks; a *belief in their inherent morality* that inclines people to ignore the ethical or moral consequences of their decisions; *collective rationalisation*, in which people discount warnings and do not question their assumptions; and *self-censorship*, by which doubts and deviations from the perceived consensus are not expressed.

In reading the Murphy Report, one cannot help being struck by the parallels with the groupthink process.

> The Dublin Archdiocese's pre-occupations in dealing with cases of child sexual abuse, at least until the mid 1990s, were the maintenance of secrecy, the avoidance of scandal, the protection of the reputation of the Church, and the preservation of its assets. All other considerations, including the welfare of children and justice for victims, were subordinated to these priorities. The Archdiocese did not implement its own canon law rules and did its best to avoid any application of the law of the State. [1.15]

No serious discussion seems to have taken place about the morality of the Church's response, about the scale and implications of the problem of abuse, about the Church's obligations under the civil law of the State, or about likely damage to its own credibility and reputation as a result of its failure to act decisively. Just as Janis wondered how such an apparently talented group of people as President Kennedy had in his cabinet could make a disastrous decision to invade Cuba at the Bay of Pigs, so one can ask how such a talented and well-meaning group of religious people could preside over the disregard and cover-up of abuse, and avoidance of responsibility for what was happening.

According to Janis, groups were particularly at risk of group-think where there was a high level of cohesion and positive self-regard among the members. It has also been observed in groups where there was a culture of fear and conformity. It could be argued that all of these were characteristic of the church hierarchy over the years. Interestingly, Janis also noted that what he called soft-hearted or caring organisations could often make very hard-hearted decisions.

Power

When we add power and an insulation from outside or opposing views to a culture that encourages groupthink, we get an enhanced possibility of very poor, heartless and dangerous decisions. Power, even by itself however, can create problems and some of these are illustrated by a very famous study in psychology called the Stanford Prison Experiment (Zimbardo, 2007). In this study, a mock prison was created in the basement of Stanford University and student volunteers were randomly assigned to be either guards or prisoners. Although scheduled to run for two weeks, the experiment was called off after five days as the guards had become too abusive and there were concerns for the well-being of the prisoners. In analysing what happened, Zimbardo made a number of observations. One is that, under certain conditions, ordinary people could be induced to commit very abusive acts. The other is that abuses were not due to the presence of 'a few bad apples' but to the culture that was created. This experiment also shows how unbridled and unaccountable power can lead to abuses of that power. Zimbardo went on to be an expert witness for the defence in the Abu Ghraib prison case where he maintained that the mistreatment of Iraqi prisoners by the US military was a systemic problem. Institutions tend to minimise responsibility by blaming such problems on isolated, abusive individuals rather than examining the role that the leadership and culture of the institution played in the abuse. Here again, in the aftermath of the Murphy Report, we see a reluctance to accept responsibility at the top of the institution and a concentration by many solely on the actual perpetrators of abuse.

In this context, there has been much focus on the auxiliary bishops who were in place at the time of the abuses highlighted in the report. Under pressure, a number offered their resignations with varying degrees of reluctance and, to date, one in particular has resisted calls for his resignation. To some extent, the issue of resignations is a distraction from much more important issues. Obviously, these have great symbolic significance and, had they been willingly offered rather than forced, would have helped repair some of the loss of credibility of the hierarchy. On the other hand, resignations, in and of themselves, do little to change the culture that created the problems. In fact, under present circumstances, it would not be a surprise if their successors became preoccupied with a rigid adherence to agreed guidelines while defensively watching their backs rather than bringing fresh, creative, more open and collaborative approaches to leadership.

The problem here is reflected in the work of Andre Gorz (1982) who maintains that in any large bureaucratic organisation, power is not a property of individuals but of the system. People do not freely define the rules or set goals but are simply agents obeying the imperatives and inertias of the system they serve.

> In modern societies, power does not have a subject. It only appears to be personal. In reality it is the effect of a structure; it derives from the existence of a machinery of domination which endows with functional power those holding positions within it, whatever the nature of their abilities or political options. As long as this machinery of domination remains intact, it is politically immaterial who the holders of positions of power may be ... The belief that the machinery of domination has to be taken over in order to subsequently change it has been a long-standing illusion of reformists.
> (Gorz, 1982, p 63).

From this point of view, changing the actors still leaves the system intact. What is needed is to change that system. Following Murphy, the challenge now is to change both the culture and the type of leadership and not just the actors. Unless the culture of distance, secrecy, restricted power and unaccountability is changed, resignations will have little effect. Unless a radically different style of leadership is adopted, the response to current and future revelations will be seriously inadequate.

Culture and social identity
In what ways is the existing culture of the Roman Catholic Church in Ireland problematic? Particular negative characteristics have already been mentioned – distant, secretive, conforming, defensive, and hierarchical, among others. A useful way to think about this, however, is in terms of the social identity of those in leadership positions and of the rest of the Church. I have written about this in depth elsewhere (Ruth 1988, 2006a), but, essentially, we can think about people as having various social identities that form the context within which they behave and interact. Some of these identities represent power and privilege. They are oppressor identities. (Calling these oppressor identities is not a judgement on the motives, intentions or goodness of those people. It is simply a description of the relationship between social groups.) Others represent being marginalised, disadvantaged, powerless, lower status and oppressed. Most of us are a mix of both oppressor and oppressed social identities. In any given context, however, some of these identities are more salient than others. They have a particular influence on what happens in that context.

In the context of the Roman Catholic Church, the leadership can be characterised as male and clerical. We could also add other characteristic identities, such as older, celibate, middle class and white, among others. It is not possible to divorce the style of leadership and the culture that has predominated from those particular identities. Essentially, we have a group of celibate, male clerics who tend to be older, middle class and white who see themselves as having the role of instructing, guiding, challenging, theorising, organising, directing and 'leading' a hugely diverse Church population that includes women, young people, victims of abuse, people of colour, lay men and women, working-class people, religious, to name but a few. And, we can also make another distinction between those who are bishops and those who are priests.

We know from studies of the processes of oppression and liberation, that communication between parties with differing identities can be problematic. In particular, it requires a special effort on the part of those with privileged, powerful or oppressor social identities when they try to listen to those with less privileged, less powerful or oppressed social identities. To engage in a listening process implies giving up some power and this is often problematic for privileged groups. Freire (1972) alluded to this when he talked about the difficulties faced by 'converts' to the people's cause, for example, people from privileged backgrounds who opt to become allies for those less privileged.

> Our converts ... truly desire to transform the unjust order; but because of their background they believe that they must be the executors of the transformation. They talk about the people but they do not trust them; and trusting the people is the indispensable precondition for revolutionary change (p 36).

What is often forgotten by dominant groups is that power is quite a unique resource. It has been said that, unlike other resources, the more it is hoarded, the smaller it gets, while the more it is given away, the greater it becomes. We can see this with the institutional Church. The more it hangs on to power, the less powerful it becomes.

Increasingly, it is apparent that the leadership of the Church is simply out of touch with the feelings, the thinking and the experiences of many of these other groups. This is not so much a criticism of the individuals in those leadership positions as it is a comment on what can happen with any dominant group that does not share power. Under present arrangements, were we to replace all of those in leadership positions, we would still have the same problems. One of the principles that has emerged from the study of processes of oppression and liberation is that it is not possible for members of a dominant, privileged or oppressor group to do the thinking for groups with a different, and, in particular, oppressed social identity. With the best will in the world, male clerics, as a group, are never going to be clear enough in their thinking to provide the necessary leadership for a diverse Church. This is not to say that individual male clerics won't have much to offer and an important role to play. What is not possible, however, is to expect that leadership can reside solely in this group and continue to be effective.

Leadership
This part of the discussion is closely related to how we understand what leadership is and what characterises true, authentic and effective leadership. There is not space here to explore in detail what we now understand about true leadership but we can highlight a number of significant features. At its core, leadership is a process of thinking about people and the situation facing them (Ruth, 1997, 2006a, 2006b). However, as we saw above in the context of social identity, there is a principle about leadership that says it is not possible to do the thinking *for* people. What is possible is to think *with* them. To do this effectively and to be able to think clearly about any situation requires a leader to *listen* to people. Real listening is something that is often espoused but less often practised. The process of listening is not just a superficial or intellectual one. Most of the important information in any situation is likely to be communicated at the level of feelings or emotions and experiences. In other words, if we ask people what they think, they will quite often tell us instead how they are feeling or what they have experienced. If we pay attention to these, we can learn an enormous amount. If we are truly to understand what is going on and what needs to happen, we have to be comfortable listening to feelings and the stories people tell about their experiences. In fact, not only do we have to be comfortable listening to these, we actively need to draw them out. At its core, leadership requires us to get in close and listen actively to what people are trying to tell us so that we get a clear picture of their struggles.

In this sense, true leadership is both a process and a type of relationship rather than a position we occupy. We can contrast it with authority. Leadership is essentially an influence relationship. It is a particular way of relating to people. Authority, on the other hand, is a position people occupy to which they have been appointed or elected. In this authority role they have been given certain responsibilities and the right to make decisions or to represent and speak on behalf of people. Ideally, those in positions of authority would also act like leaders. Often this does not happen. However, when it does happen, an interesting thing occurs. As they take leadership, they come to rely less and less on the trappings of authority. On the other hand, where authority and leadership do not go together, the person in authority tends to resort more and more to those trappings. They insist on their right to command, to decide things unilaterally, to be obeyed, to be treated with deference, and so on. In effect, authority without leadership quickly becomes authoritarian. In order to avoid this happening, authority has to embody leadership and, as we have seen, this entails active listening. The challenge for Church leaders now is to move from occupying positions of authority to building those influence relationships.

The model of leadership that we have seen highlighted by Murphy, and by many of the events before and since its publication, is that of a hierarchical, distant and defensive style that drew little on listening to those not in leadership. Because of the huge outcry generated by the revelations in Murphy and other reports, bishops have been forced to engage in a process of listening and dialogue with victims and the groups representing them. This has been fraught with tension and conflict at various times and still has a long way to go. It has happened, not because bishops saw it as a central part of their role as leaders, but because it was demanded of them. And, following the outcry over what was revealed, while they have claimed to be listening, victims and their representatives have not felt listened to. Something is missing in this process and this needs to be thought about. In addition, other groups in the Church, such as women and young people, are also signalling their disaffection.

Communication and change

At this point, we can return to the discussion of social identities. Listening, as we have seen, does not take place in a vacuum. It takes place between individuals and groups with particular identities. For a powerful, privileged group such as the bishops to get this process right, we can draw on some guidelines. A starting point is that real change rarely comes from the direction of those with power or privilege. As we saw earlier, as a group, it is unlikely that they will be able to understand clearly what is going on and what needs to happen and unlikely that they will be sufficiently motivated to make any kind of radical changes. This is not to say that individual priests or bishops will not have great clarity and commitment to change, but the group as a whole is unlikely to change on its own. For real change to happen, it is necessary to listen to those who are oppressed, marginalised or underprivileged within the existing culture.

Given the salient identities referred to earlier – male, clerical, older, white, etc. – we can point to the corresponding identities as crucial to any process of change. This means there is a pressing need for bishops and clergy, both individually and formally as a group, to engage in a deep listening process with women, lay people, young people, people of colour, working-class people and other groups with particular social identities. It will not be possible for the bishops and clergy to change the existing culture on their own. A useful attitude for someone from a privileged background to adopt in a listening process such as this is to assume that, coming from their background, they just don't 'get it' and that the real expertise and understanding lies with the other group. This makes it less likely that they will be pulled into making pronouncements about other people or pretending to understand or empathise more than they actually do. Starting from such a humble position can make very real dialogue possible.

Such a listening process could take place in a series of parish, diocesan and national assemblies or synods. To begin with, these could create a space for people who share the same social identity to listen to each other's thoughts, feelings and experiences as members of the Church. Groups with different social identities (for example, priests, lay people, young people and bishops) could then come together to learn about each other, think together about the struggles and challenges facing them and the kinds of support they need from each other, and plan together how to build a Church that reflects their deepest aspirations.

Priests
The abuses highlighted in Murphy are also pointing to a much wider problem facing priests, as men. The revelations of inadequate responses to abuse that Murphy has highlighted are re-

flected also in the hierarchy's response to other problems. When, for example, the secret lives of Bishop Casey and Fr Cleary became public, this was a clear signal that a problem existed in relation to celibacy and the involvement of clergy in sexual relationships. Rather than facing this, however, and beginning a process of listening to priests and to lay people involved with priests about their relationships and the quality of their lives, the problem was again reduced to the failings of particular individuals rather than a systemic one. This issue still has not been addressed to any great degree. The pattern in these situations has been to play down their significance, intervene only when forced to and pay little regard to the damage done to those hurt or scandalised in the process. At some point, a question has to be asked about whether the type of life that priests are expected to have is either healthy or sustainable in human terms.

The issue here is not simply about celibacy, which may or may not be appropriate in certain situations or for certain periods. It is clear, however, that requiring people to live lives lacking in closeness or intimacy and with high levels of isolation does not make sense. One response under such circumstances is to substitute sex for closeness but in ways that may be deeply damaging to women and children and other men. If they are to be an effective resource in today's world, priests must have lives that meet basic human needs for closeness and intimacy and their formation programmes should contain a much greater focus on relationships, sexuality, gender and sexism. It is time to recognise and address the real struggles and the pastoral and human needs of priests. The problems we are seeing, apart from the deep hurt and damage they have caused to those affected, are also like a red flag drawing attention to a much wider problem affecting men in the Church. It should also be said that addressing the struggles faced by priests would ideally go hand in hand with addressing the position of women in the Church. The listening process described above would be one setting where these issues might be raised.

Conclusion
The Murphy Report has revealed a shocking litany of abuses and cover-ups. The bishops have a range of choices in where

they go from here. They could adopt a head-in-the-sand approach and wait for the controversy to blow over while making minimalist changes. In this regard, there is a mindset that says the Church has been around for 2000 years and it will survive periods like this. On the other hand, they could recognise the huge mistakes that have been made, accept responsibility for them and implement robust procedures to ensure the protection of young people in future. Or, they could go further and recognise the need for a broad renewal process that alters significantly the relationship between bishops, priests and lay people and the ways in which leadership in the Church is exercised.

I hear many clergy and religious groups talking about a crisis of identity and wondering what their mission is in the Ireland of today. By recognising and cherishing the diversity of the Church and identifying all the significant identities that make up this diversity, a new mission can be forged. Part of this mission should be to build close, supportive relationships within and between the various identities, to identify their respective struggles, and to work together to eliminate all forms of inequality and oppression. It is in this context that the Church can restore its credibility and ensure that abuses such as we have seen will not be repeated.

Works Cited
Freire, P. (1972), *Pedagogy of the Oppressed*, Harmondsworth: Penguin.
Gorz, A. (1982), *Farewell to the Working Class: An Essay on Post-Industrial Socialism*, London: Pluto Press.
Janis, I. L. (1972), *Victims of Groupthink*, Boston. Houghton Mifflin.
Ruth, S. (1997), 'Leadership in the Church', in *The Furrow*, 48 (6), June, 327-33.
Ruth, S. (1988), 'Understanding Oppression and Liberation', in *Studies*, 77 (308), 434-44.
Ruth, S. (2006a), *Leadership and Liberation: A Psychological Approach*, London: Routledge.
Ruth, S. (2006b), *High-Quality Leadership: A Self-Assessment Guide for Individuals and Teams*, Dublin: Veritas.
Zimbardo, P. (2007), *The Lucifer Effect: How Good People Turn Evil*, London: Rider.

CHAPTER ELEVEN

The Murphy and Ryan Reports: Between Evangelising and Priesthood

Enda McDonagh

Given the spate of commentary on and of proposals for Church reform which have followed the Ryan and Murphy Reports of 2009, there is bound to be little new to say or to write. Indeed, the time for saying and writing is long past. Now is the time for doing. However radical the doing ought to be, (and radical it ought to be) it ought not to be impulsive or, above all, un-thought out. The danger of that precaution is however that it may defer the doing and excuse the deferring.

In what might appear a very unfortunate conjunction, the major exposures of clerical and religious sexual abuse of children overlap with the years designated by the Church as the years of Evangelisation and for the Priest. This chapter will attempt to relate in potentially positive ways the horrors of the exposed sexual abuse and the scandal of its inexcusable cover-up with the thrust of these Christian callings to Evangelisation and Priesthood. How far that is possible remains to be discovered.

I. Evangelisation and the priority of the abused
Words, even words intending or describing action, can be burdensome and opaque, retarding the action or at least misdirecting it. 'Evangelisation' is one of these words. Perhaps its Latin connections ending in '-ation' share similar burdens and opacity. In current discourse, 'nationalisation' (of banks, etc.), 'homogenisation' of endless materials and 'rationalisation' of jobs might serve as examples. 'Evangelisation' has its particular difficulties as a word and as a proposed or attempted practice. As a word it echoes for many not '*evangelium*', gospel or good news but the 'proselytising' attempts by power-seeking (and wealth-seeking), individuals or sects to draw more and more people into their congregations and spheres of influence. American

tele-evangelists are the most notorious example of this type of evangelisation.

The methods usually involve the carrot of health or wealth or happiness here and hereafter and the stick of suffering or poverty or punishment now and eternal punishment hereafter. The Christian Right in politics, which may indeed be right on some particular issues, is deeply implicated with this type of worldly and basically unChristian 'evangelisation'. To renew and resource the authentic Christian model we must return to the *evangelium* itself, to the gospel, to Jesus. His person, his message and his ministry as they led to his passion, death and resurrection must be our guide. This is a life-long task in word and deed for every disciple.

In their comments on their recent meeting with the Pope (15-16 February 2010) the Irish bishops said that the priority of all was the suffering of the abused. Rooted in Jesus' ministry to the poor, the sick and the excluded which culminated in his laying down of his life for all, this may be the correct starting point for the present-day Church's mission of preaching the gospel, of evangelising, a less leaden word than evangelisation. Many of the gospel expressions of such evangelising in word and deed were repeated in modern times in papal encyclicals, in the famous phrase of the 1971 Roman Synod about justice seeking as a constituent part of preaching the gospel, in the writings and doings of liberation theologians and in the many contemporary movements of justice and peace. The fruit of all these is still maturing but they provide a nourishing context for a campaign of evangelising that would today focus on the victims of clerical and religious abuse.

Such focus should begin by getting to know the victims, not just representatives, but as many as possible, not in merely official and formal terms but in growing friendship. This is a responsibility not just of bishops, too isolated from the broader Church, but of clergy, religious and lay Catholics in their own locality or range of contacts. Only in this way will some effective understanding of the lives and sufferings of the abused be achieved and an adequate human and Christian response become possible. What this implies is that bishops and the wider Church must first be evangelised by the abused, brought to some deeper and fuller meaning of the gospel by the abused before they presume to lead in the evangelising of others. By placing themselves in this way, humbly, at the disposition of the abused, upon whom of course they have no claim of acceptance, they are already proclaiming the gospel of Jesus Christ. It was he who, in the words of Paul to the Philippians, 'though he was in the form of God, did not count equality with God a thing to be grasped, but emptied himself, taking the form of a servant, being born in the likeness of men. And being found in human form he humbled himself and became obedient unto death, even death on a cross' (Phil 2:6-9). His self-emptying example must undergird our approach to the sexually abused.

All of this has implications for the elevated and isolated, if not luxurious, lifestyle, and even the dress of bishop-servants and other clergy. Beyond the externals lie the calls to repentance and reconciliation. The mood and manner of repentance by bishops and clergy will emerge as they seek integration with the abused but integration will have to be worked at and takes time. More serious difficulties may lie in seeking to help the abusers to find repentance and reconciliation and in supporting the abused in responding to them. Generous financial and other recompense to the abused and their families must continue and in time may help to bring clerical abusers through repentance and restitution to reconciliation. In this context justice must be seen to be done and done as graciously as possible. Bishops and clergy who have been unfairly or ungraciously treated should, with the support of their confrères and lay friends, also seek to be evangelised by the abused to find again the peace of Christ.

II. The call for Church reform: Honouring the priesthood of baptism and sharing the priesthood of ordination

The message of the Year for the Priest has been both narrowly and unfortunately focused on the ordained, narrowly because it has overlooked the broader and prior priesthood of baptism, and unfortunately because, as noted above, it overlaps with the reports on clerical and religious sexual and physical abuse of children. Indeed such a narrow perception of priesthood confined to ordained and celibate males has almost certainly contributed to the clerical scandals and only its proper setting in the context of the broader priesthood of the faithful will enable the Church to confront seriously its current problems. In passing it may be said that any attempt to reduce these problems to managerial and communication issues is destined for disaster, even though there have been atrocious failures in management and communication at the level of Church leadership.

For too many Catholics, conservative, liberal and radical (whatever these terms may really mean), the Vatican, its documents and proposed reforms evoke only a tiresome sigh. This is due in part to past failings. Without entering into the continuing controversies about collegiality, liturgical reform or ecumenical paralysis, this brief essay will try to re-imagine the new vision of Church which the documents of Vatican II offer us in the present crisis. I say re-imagine because the 'according to the letter' interpretations are too controverted and because 2010 provides quite different ecclesial and social contexts and challenges to Church and world from those evident in the years 1962 to 1965. For our purposes, the context of clerical sex abuse presents the most immediate challenge but it too grew out of slower and deeper infections in Church and society. Many of these preceded the Council but were unknown, ignored or inadequately diagnosed / discerned and treated.

What did clearly emerge at the Council, and is still broadly accepted, was a theological vision of the Church in its many dimensions. In their primary mysterious or mystical qualities, they might be listed for our task as follows: the mystery of God's presence in the world; the People of God; the Body of Christ; the Dwelling Place or Temple of the Holy Spirit; the Community of Disciples. To these visions of Church (and others might be included) structures of service in prayer, teaching and care, must conform and by these be reformed. Structured as they have been in different ways over time, the services of prayer, teaching and care remain in diverse fashions the call and gift of all members of the Church, of all the believing and baptised.

This variety of visions and images of the Church, with their biblical, patristic and traditional roots, were given new life through Vatican II and its transcending of the dominant institutional and hierarchical models of the previous centuries. Not that the visions were ever entirely absent but they were too frequently ignored or obscured in the lazy identification of Church with institution and of institution simply with its leaders, the pope and the bishops. These latter remain essential parts of the structure of the Church. How they are understood and operate must be considered after the major conciliar documents in the context of the Church as the mystery of God's presence and, particularly for our purposes, as the People of God, the community of baptised believers. The priesthood of baptism then is the setting in which the priesthood of ordination, sacerdotal and episcopal, must be understood and exercised. Ordained priests and bishops come from, belong within and are called to the service of the priestly people. Any suggestion of their lording it over them is a clear betrayal of the gospel, and so are many of the symbols of power and superiority which are still in vogue. The angry reaction of many Irish Catholics (especially women) to the Irish bishops deferentially bowing to kiss the pope's ring (the power-symbol of the *servus servorum Dei*) was undoubtedly unexpected but in the end excusable. More offensive still are the more inhibiting gestures and actions of dominance-subservience which characterise and eventually tend to corrupt pope-bishop, bishop-priest, and clergy-laity relationships. And the price of all that? Recognisable in part in the clerical abuse scandal as young people were afraid to resist or report; parents, teachers and others unwilling to believe. And bishops? Scampering to cover up, to protect the ordained against the most vulnerable of the baptised. If bishops and other clergy are to recover moral authority and religious leadership, they must resume their place among the baptised, honouring the priority of that sacrament which has been traditionally accepted as *radix et fundamentum*, the root and foundation of all Christian existence.

The People of God which forms the company and companionship of the disciples of Christ has, by his word and example and under the guidance of the Holy Spirit, continued to develop its structures from the New Testament to the present. The development is by no means complete. Even essential elements listed above such as bishops and pope have changed over the centuries. The manner of episcopal appointment has changed radically in recent centuries away from local involvement to centralisation in the Vatican. The episcopal range of duties has become almost exclusively administrative. Forms of episcopal relationship with others have become, as already noted, more subservient to Rome and more dominant within their dioceses. The style and substance of episcopal services to the community, as well as the personalities of bishops themselves, have reflected these fluctuations in structure over the centuries.

At their best, developments in structures have been prompted by both the mission-needs of the Church and the saving needs of the world at any particular time. Crises in Church and world have been the great challenges. At their worst the developments have been prompted by fear of a changing world. Political opportunism and power-seeking by churchmen and statesmen have also exercised their baneful influence from time to time. The Church as would-be communion of saints has too often proved to be dominantly a communion of sinners, as any acquaintance with Church history readily demonstrates.

The crisis of clerical and religious sex abuse of children has roots, in the universal Church as well as the Irish Church, deeper than the sexual failures of individual priests and religious or the failures in supervisory responsibility of individual popes and bishops. That is why no simple change or improvement in management can be adequate or even effective in the longer term. Only by re-imagining the Church, its structures and personnel and their operations in terms of the biblical model of Jesus, his followers and disciples, can we hope to uncover the deeper pathologies and discover their effective treatment. In all this the recovery of the dominant biblical images such as People of God, Body of Christ and Temple of the Holy Spirit among others and their practical implications will be primary.

This re-imaging is initiated and sustained by the Holy Spirit who is to lead us into the fuller truth and keep us faithful in our renewed practices. Spirit-filled fidelity, imagination and experimentation will be the characteristics of urgent Church renewal in this 'process', as it has been called by many bishops on their return from Rome The urgency of the crisis requires an immediate start to that process. This should involve their listening and learning among the whole People of God. They should recognise their intimate and reciprocal relations with all the members of the Body of Christ (if one member suffers all suffer), and oc-

cupy in that mode the back pews of the Temple of the Holy
Spirit. How otherwise is the Spirit to activate the gifts he has
showered on all in baptism and confirmation?

For almost twenty years now a national consultative assembly
has been promoted by at least one bishop and a range of priests,
as well as by theologians and lay members for the Irish Catholic
Church, in response to the growing crisis. If it had been acted on
ten years ago, as it might, the crisis would not have escalated to
its present proportions. No point in lamenting but there is point
in learning that only the involvement of the whole believing and
baptised community will help now. Such involvement will demand conversion of mind and heart, of relationship and activity
in all Church circles. (I almost said 'at all levels' just when we are
trying to get beyond levels, although 'circles' with its 'inner' and
'outer', has its own exclusivist ring, a ring hollow to gospel
ears.)

How this is to be best and most urgently achieved requires
the exercise of these gifts of the Spirit in fidelity, imagination
and experimentation. Groups of lay-people have already begun
their own informal consultation. They might expand to parish or
area inviting the clergy to join but not handing over. The local
bishop might ask to be allowed to join such groups as a humble
participant but not merely listening and then departing to make
the decisions on his own or in some clerical context. There is no
simple, single approach which will work everywhere for everybody. In fact, there may be no totally successful approach at all
whereby genuine dialogue and consultative decision making is
truly faithful to the workings of the Spirit and truly responsive
to the dimensions of the crisis – the ambiguity of the Church in
history continues. The Reign of God is not yet complete. So the
efforts of faith-filled imagination and experimentation will have
to go on. The more urgent goal is a national Church consultation
or assembly. This, at its ambiguous best, may yield a provisional
programme on the best practices and structures for the present
and no doubt continuing crises.

There are many related questions which have often been
aired only to be ignored in the past. How can the Spirit of ordination, for example, be confined to male celibates if the present
clerical culture is to be banished? Is there any real theological

justification for the exclusion of women from the ordained priesthood? When will the Church escape from the strait-jacket of *Humanae Vitae* to develop a genuine theology of sexuality? And how is Christianity to remain credible if it refuses to learn from the secular world and its many valid insights, particularly in regard to communications, social structures and the fuller recognition of human rights within and without the Church itself? Important progress has been made on some aspects of these issues at Vatican II and in later encyclicals, but too much has been ignored or repressed. Some of that failure is theological as theologians, out of fear (too often justified) or false loyalty, have refused the intellectual challenges or prophetic roles taken on by some of their predecessors. Theology in Ireland has frequently suffered from such failures. As long as it does the faithful, imaginative and courageous renewal of the Irish Church will be no more than another cover-up.

CHAPTER TWELVE

Broken Hearts and not just Torn Garments – Beginning the Discussion about Forgiveness and Healing

Eamonn Conway

Introduction

I first became aware of Child Sexual Abuse while working as a priest at a place of pilgrimage in Ireland in the early nineties. Occasionally, pilgrims spoke about having been sexually abused as children. Generally, the abuse had been perpetrated by a member of their own family: by their father, step-father or older brother; incredibly on some occasions by more than one family member.

I remember experiencing anger and deep sadness that they could think that the criminal violent actions of others had somehow made them feel impure before God and themselves. I remember finding it so difficult to help them to believe that they were utterly precious to God and loved by God, and that God cared deeply about their pain and violation. I also remember feeling so grateful that I had grown up in a home where I had felt safe and loved; something I had until then taken utterly for granted.

I remember being particularly shocked and outraged the first time I was told of sexual abuse perpetrated by a priest. The priest was long since deceased but the pain and hurt which the victim had carried through her teen years and into adulthood had marked and marred every significant moment and aspect of her life: dating, marriage, sexuality, her relationships with her husband and children. It seems surprising that some of those who were abused by priests for some reason need to talk to a priest and to have it confirmed and acknowledged by a priest that the abuse was utterly wrong and was something for which they had no culpability.

I relate these experiences for three reasons. The first is that it is sometimes forgotten that many priests, along with other caring professionals, have been quietly helping victims of sexual abuse as part of their day-to-day ministry.

Second, it is important that we do not approach child sexual abuse as an abstract problem. We are speaking of evil, immoral, criminal acts that have damaged and in some cases destroyed innocent people, acts all the more perverse because they have been committed by ordained ministers of the gospel.

Third, this particular story illustrates that initially many victims of sexual abuse by clergy have wanted very little. They have wanted to be listened to and believed. They have needed to hear from someone in authority that the abuse should not have happened, and that it was not in any way their fault. They have also wanted, if the sexual offender was still alive, to be reassured that he is not still in a position to abuse others.

Betrayal of trust by offender and *by institution*
The sad reality is that for several victims of abuse by clergy the little they wanted proved to be too much. The horrific violation which they experienced at the hands of their priest sexual offender was compounded by some Church authorities in their failure to respond appropriately and with pastoral sensitivity.

In my limited experience, sexual abuse is fundamentally about betrayal of trust and abuse of power. I will return later to the issue of power.

With regard to the betrayal of trust, it has to be borne in mind that very often victims knew and admired the priest and gave freely to him their child-like and innocent confidence, a trust and confidence that was utterly exploited, manipulated, shattered and betrayed. We must recall here, and bear in mind when we make comparisons with abuse by other professionals, that priests have been the most privileged among the caring professions, with responsibility for and perceived authority over the spiritual wellbeing of their people. For this reason, clergy sex abusers have been referred to as 'slayers of the soul'.[1]

In the Irish context, account must also be taken of the virtually unassailable position which the priest held in a society in which almost everyone was 'churched'. In retrospect, it may seem surprising that the Garda Síochána were so deferential towards clergy and Church authorities, but it wasn't at the time.

---

1. See Stephen J. Rossetti, *A Tragic Grace: The Catholic Church and Child Sexual Abuse* (Minnesota: Collegeville, 1996).

To bring home the point about the unique damage sexual abuse by a priest can do, one trauma expert, when addressing the landmark meeting of the US Bishops' Conference in Dallas in 2002, went so far as to describe child sexual abuse by a priest as a form of incest:

> Make no mistake about it. The sexual violation of a child or adolescent by a priest *is* incest. It is a sexual and relational transgression perpetrated by *the* father of the child's extended family; a man in whom the child is taught from birth to trust above everyone else in his life, to trust second only to God. Priest abuse *is* incest.[2]

Horrific as sexual abuse was, for many victims, the response they experienced from office-holders when they eventually found the courage to come forward and speak of their abuse was a further, and in some cases, an even more profound betrayal of trust. Words one victim has used to describe her treatment include: cold, defensive, being lied to; threatened, legalistic, being directed to a solicitor; being told that she probably had been to blame for her abuser's actions; being considered a nuisance, a threat and the enemy.[3]

The one thing pastors should have been good at – responding pastorally to someone hurting and in need – some of them got tragically wrong. The response of office holders in such diverse places as Poznan in Poland, Boston in the USA, or Ferns, and now Dublin in Ireland, has been a shameful saga of putting the perceived needs of the institution first and, for the most part, a disregard not only for the legal rights of and justice for the victims, but also for their pastoral care and well-being. I say 'perceived needs of the institution', because the genuine needs of an institution which is at the service of the gospel can only be met if

2. Mary Gail Frawley-O'Dea, 'The long-term impact of sexual trauma'. Paper presented to the National Conference of Catholic Bishops, Dallas, Texas, 13 June 2002, p 2 (her emphases). According to the Sexual Abuse and Violence in Ireland (SAVI) Report, clerical/religious ministers or clerical/religious teachers constitute 3.2% of known child sexual abusers. However, some clergy and religious tend to have more victims than relatives or other authority figure categories.
3. Marie Collins, 'Breaking the Silence: the Victims', in *Concilium* 2004/3, pp 15ff.

every action taken in its name is characterised by justice, truth, and love. The betrayal of victims was a betrayal of the Church as well.

There is a striking similarity between the findings of investigations conducted by civil authorities in the archdioceses of Dublin and in Boston: catastrophic errors of judgement by those in leadership; a primary concern for secrecy and the avoidance of scandal; the subordination of the needs of victims to institutional self-protection.[4] These are damning findings, and there are more to come. Internationally, historic cases of sexual abuse in ecclesial contexts are emerging with greater frequency, including in non-English speaking contexts, dispelling the myth that this is a matter peculiar to the emigrant Irish–influenced English-speaking world.

So where do we go from here?
The Ferns, Ryan and Murphy Reports have utterly vindicated victims. They would seem to have gone some way to compensating for the experience of not having been believed, listened to and responded to in a spirit of openness, transparency and accountability by Church authorities.

Anyone who commits a criminal act should face the full rigours of the criminal process. That said, there are some ways in which legal processes fall short. In some instances, cases cannot be brought against offenders because of the statutes of limitation or the absence of evidence. Victims have also demanded some legal action against authorities who, by their actions or inaction, allowed sexual abuse to continue. However, as the Murphy Report points out, the crime of misprision of felony does not apply to sexual abuse misdemeanours.

Beyond these limitations of the legal justice system, the issue of healing remains. Can legal processes alone deliver healing? Only victims can really answer that, and to what extent, at the end of the day, healing is a personal matter which only those hurt can ultimately address. Arguably, however, something more is needed from the Church's perspective. So what is on offer from

---

4. Compare The Murphy Report [1.1110 and 1.15] with the Report of the Office of the Attorney General of the Commonwealth of Massachusetts (2003).

Church leadership since the publication of the Murphy Report? At the time of writing we still await the Apostolic Letter from Pope Benedict. However, in my view, the recent statements from Irish bishops and from the Holy See seem to have moved things on a little. It must also be stated that the solution to the problems facing the Irish Church lie within the Irish Church.

There is recognition by the Irish bishops of a failure of moral leadership and accountability (9 December 2009). There is expression of deep shock at the scale and depravity of the abuse. There is explicit acknowledgement of cover-up and of the fact that 'the avoidance of scandal, the preservation of the reputations of individuals and of the Church, took precedence over the safety and welfare of children.' The bishops accept that 'this should never have happened and must never be allowed to happen again.' The bishops also say that 'the Report raises very important issues for the Church in Ireland, including the functioning of the Bishops' Conference, and how the lay faithful can be more effectively involved in the life of the Church.' They promise to give further detailed consideration to these issues. The statement concludes by stating: 'We humbly ask for forgiveness.' I will return to this.

On 11 December 2009, Pope Benedict met Cardinal Brady and Archbishop Martin. In the statement issued afterwards we are told that

'the Holy Father was deeply disturbed and distressed by the contents of the Murphy Report and that he expressed once more his profound regret at the actions of some members of the clergy who have betrayed their solemn promises to God, as well as the trust placed in them by the victims and their families, and by society at large.'

The statement issued on 16 February 2010, following the meeting of the Irish bishops with the Holy See, acknowledges the breakdown in trust in the Church's leadership and the damage to the Church's mission. We are told that the Pope requested the bishops 'to address the problems of the past with determination and resolve, and to face the present crisis with honesty and courage.' The Pope, we are also told, 'stressed the need for a deeper theological reflection on the whole issue'.

In each of their statements, the bishops have also been anxious to point out that best practice has been introduced in terms of child protection in the Church at all levels.

Broken hearts and not just torn garments
The Pope has asked that the past be faced with determination and resolve, and the present with honesty and courage. The Irish bishops have specifically asked for forgiveness. It seems to me that these statements are not insignificant and that they do provide the basis for embarking upon a process which might eventually deliver healing to the victims, forgiveness to the sexual offenders and office-holders, and reconciliation and renewal to the people of God. The problem is that we have to get things right the first time because to embark on a process half-heartedly or insincerely, and to fail, would be yet another case of catastrophic abuse.

Best practice with regard to the protection of children, greater involvement of the lay faithful in the life of the Church, better screening practices for candidates for the priesthood, continuing formation for clergy, and hopefully also for bishops, restructuring of dioceses and so on, are important considerations. But addressing systems issues in the Church, while important, is not going to be enough. One of our key Lenten texts instructs us that true repentance requires not just attention to the externals, a rending of our clothing, but also of our hearts (Joel 2: 13).

So can we begin to talk about a process of repentance leading to forgiveness? Nietzche had little time for forgiveness, considering it a form of 'sublimated resentment' and the last resort of the loser. By contrast, the Christian understanding is that true forgiveness brings us to a situation in which we no longer speak in terms of losers or winners, because all parties are restored to their most true and authentic selves.[5]

Desmond Tutu, who had just cause to approach the concept of forgiveness with caution, has written:

5. See Eugene Duffy, 'Forgiveness and Reconciliation', in Eamonn Conway, Eugene Duffy, Attracta Shields (eds), *The Church and Child Sexual Abuse – Towards a Pastoral Response* (Dublin: The Columba Press, 1999), p 68; see further, Eamonn Conway, 'The Service of a Different Kingdom: Child Sexual Abuse and the Response of the Church', p 87.

Forgiving and being reconciled to our enemies or our loved ones is not about pretending that things are other than they are. It is not about patting one another on the back and turning a blind eye to the wrong. True reconciliation exposes the awfulness, the abuse, the pain, the hurt, the truth. It could even sometimes make things worse. It is a risky undertaking, but in the end it is worthwhile, because in the end dealing with the real situation helps to bring real healing. Superficial reconciliation can bring only superficial healing.[6]

Some years ago a sexual abuse victim asked me to arrange a meeting for her with her priest abuser and to accompany her. After much preparation we met in a neutral space with a facilitator and a support person for each party. It was intended to be a once-off encounter during which the victim would first speak and the offender would then respond. The victim spoke so powerfully that I was reminded of the story in Luke's gospel of the woman bent double who, when healed, is able to stand up straight (Lk 13:10-17). I could sense her recover her sense of inner strength and power as the meeting progressed. At the same time, the offender began to lose his grip over her and also became increasingly visibly disturbed and pained as he was presented with incontrovertible testimony about the decades of damage his abuse had caused.

It was meant to be a once-off meeting but the facilitator wisely decided that any immediate response by the abuser would be likely to fail the sincerity test, and be of little help to the victim. The abuser needed to sit with what he had heard; to allow her words to sear into the depths of his heart. For the victim – now survivor – significant healing seemed to me to have happened by virtue of her having confronted her abuser and having recovered her inner power; to an extent his words were going to be of relative importance only. When we met a month later, however, it was clear that the abuser had also done a lot of growing and that he was also a different man.

I believe that such encounters can be healing with regard to abuse not only by sexual offenders, but by the office-holders in

6. Desmond Tutu, *God Has a Dream: A Vision of Hope for Our Time* (London: Ebury Press, 2004), pp 55-56.

the Church as well. I know that there have already been many meetings between victims and Church leaders, with varying degrees of success, and perhaps both sides, bishops and victims, are weary of such encounters at this stage. It seems to me, however, that qualitatively different encounters are needed along the lines I have suggested here, in which there is space to expose the full awfulness of what has happened and without recourse to the solace of immediate words or gestures of apology. These meetings would also need to be kept separate from any processes aimed at reaching legal settlements and compensation.

I believe such encounters could be transformative both for the victims and for the Church. Understandably, given the double betrayal of trust victims have already experienced, victims might reasonably be very reluctant to go down this road and need considerable reassurance regarding the intentions and integrity of those who would be taking part.

It must be acknowledged that not all victims wish to confront their abusers. However, in terms of building trust and demonstrating that a change of heart has taken place, it would seem essential that priests, whose lack of acceptance of past wrongdoing is still causing pain and hurt to victims, would be called upon to admit to their crimes. Similarly, bishops who have seriously mishandled cases, and thus caused further damage to victims, should also acknowledge this now, rather than do so only subsequently and under external pressure. Bishops and other office-holders would need to listen to how their actions or inaction affected victims. They would need to be afforded an opportunity to speak of the complexities they faced in decision-making and of how they felt they were prepared and resourced for their role, and the supports they had available to them while exercising their office.[7]

On one occasion Desmond Tutu had to point out to a victim that 'much and all as God loves you, he equally loves your enemy.'[8] Difficult and unpalatable as it may be to consider,

---

7. See Colm O'Reilly, 'The Dilemma of those in authority', in Eamonn Conway, Eugene Duffy, Attracta Shields (eds), *The Church and Child Sexual Abuse*, pp 61-66.
8. Tutu, *God Has a Dream*, p 41.

there is a duty of care to all those who have done wrong and this would have to be recognised in the process.

Taking up the Pope's invitation to deep theological reflection it seems to me that a national Church body, consisting of experts in theology and other relevant disciplines, but also with a wide variety of life experience, should be instituted to read and consider the implications of the recent State investigations for the mission and life of the Church in Ireland into the future. In particular this body should reflect upon the following:

- Those who sexually abuse do so out of a deep sense of their own inner powerlessness. We must ensure that priests and bishops are enabled to exercise their power and authority in a manner that is appropriate to the gospel and is deeply respectful; and that all exercises of authority are experienced as empowering and enabling. What steps do we need to take to ensure that the only power that is exercised in the Church is the power of the cross, a power that is manifest only in humble service?

- Celibacy as such is not a cause of sexual abuse by priests. However, those who are psychosexually immature may find mandatory celibacy appealing as a way of avoiding having to deal with their sexuality. We have to consider the issue of mandatory celibacy, if only in order to ensure that the charism is lived fully and joyfully by those who have commited to it. We need to help especially diocesan priests to have a mature and viable spiritual understanding of celibacy as a charism, and not just provide them with coping mechanisms.

- We need theological consideration of what the *sensus fidelium* means in practice, and of how we understand the presence and activity of the Spirit manifesting itself in the life of the faithful. As dioceses begin to look to their people to help meet the costs of compensating victims it is to be expected that people will demand greater and more transparent forms of accountability. We need to look at how, in accordance with the bishops' acknowledgment of the need for a greater involvement of the lay faithful in the life of the Church, appropriate forms of horizontal accountability can be instituted.

- One could also speak of operative theologies of priesthood[9] and what the Second Vatican Council had to say regarding sin in the Church, so that we come to a theologically solid understanding of both individual and corporate responsibility.

These are some of the issues which, taking up the Pope's invitation, need to be faced with honesty and courage. What is most important is an assurance at the outset that the disposition of those who engage in this process is one of trust in and commitment to discovering and accepting the truth. In this regard we need to ensure that there are no unnecessary 'no-go' areas. On the one hand, we must consider issues such as greater lay participation and how power and decision-making are exercised in the Church. On the other, Pope Benedict's observation that the sexual abuse of minors is connected with the weakening of faith and a general lack of respect for the human person, should also be taken seriously, and certainly not dismissed, as it was, without any effort having been made to understand what he was saying.

Conclusion

The reality is that child sexual abuse is widespread in society. At least now we have a context in the Church in which victims of abuse by priests can come forward with the assurance of being heard and responded to appropriately and professionally. We can also expect that priests are being better screened, trained and, hopefully, supported, and that children are being protected as far as is humanly possible. We can also hope that bishops will also be better prepared and resourced for their responsibilities.

Where the Church is concerned, the credible presentation of Christian faith, the very possibility of Christian faith as an option for the next generation, depends upon our ability to become reconciled with those we have offended. In this regard, much remains to be done. Healing, forgiveness, reconciliation, and the rebuilding of trust are going to take time, effort, great skill and, above all, conversion of heart.

This is not a time for harsh or harmful words (Eph 4:29). Attention needs to be paid to reconciliation within the Church

---

9. See Eamonn Conway, 'Operative Theologies of Priesthood: Have they Contributed to Child Sexual Abuse?', in *Concilium* 2004/3, pp 72-86.

where not just unity between bishops but communion between the faithful, priests and bishops has been deeply wounded. Traditionally, the reconciliation of wrongdoers was considered the work of the whole Church. Indeed, the primary purpose of canonical penance was to enlist the intercession of the whole community for the penitents. There is no doubt that the reconciliation and renewal of the Church will only be effected through the prayerful and practical co-operation of all the People of God.

Finally, we need to realise that while repentance is indispensable, ultimately forgiveness cannot be earned: it is always experienced as an unconditional gift which usually arises from the recognition and acceptance of the gratuitousness and abundance of God's merciful love.

CHAPTER THIRTEEN

A Personal View of a Communications Failure in a Time of Crisis

Eddie Shaw

'And you shall know the truth, and the truth shall make you free.' (Jn 8:32)
'The truth is rarely pure and never simple.' (Oscar Wilde, in *The Importance of being Earnest*)

We live in interesting times – a cliché that has come into its own in recent years. The world is a vastly different place than it was just twelve or twenty-four months ago. Governments, politicians, civil servants, business people and religious leaders the world over are struggling to find solutions and ways forward. Whatever the primary cause of the implosion, one fact seems clear. From the public to private sector, from industry to services, from regulated to regulator, from boardroom to battle ground, from Church to congregation, from every compass point there is a converging view that professional standards have suffered a systemic failure, with potentially catastrophic consequences.

It is now clear to leaders and to many others that the primary cause of this near collapse of the Western capitalist (and social) system is a chronic failure in decision-making, a failure to apply the values which leaders claimed to practice, a basic failure among leaders to know and apply the difference between right and wrong, to put long-term sustainability before short-term financial gain. What makes this recent cycle of failure stand out is the scale of failure, the breadth and depth of the consequences and, as we now also know, the longevity of the failure. Only time and analysis will expose the extent of the failure; new leaders will provide the lessons for others to rebuild a hope-filled and sustainable future.

Standing out, on this island, in the centre of these market failures and personal failures is the abominable fact and crime of abuse and neglect of children. According to the SAVI (Sexual Abuse and Violence in Ireland) Report 2002 we are informed that abuse of children as defined in that report is relatively common and that no part of our society is exempt. The vast majority of such abuse is delivered within the family network or by family friends or acquaintances, about ninety seven out of one hundred perpetrators fall within this category. According to the same report 'clerical/religious ministers or clerical/religious teachers constituted 3.2% of abusers' (or three out of one hundred using the same expression of the measure). It is this latter incidence that has been reported on in the Ryan and the Murphy Reports (The Murphy Report of the Commission of Investigation into the handling of allegations of child sexual abuse by priests of the Dublin Archdiocese 1975-2004.) There is no equivalent published documentation on other abuse, abuse which continues today in our community and is reported on with depressing frequency and detail.

The sexual and violent abuse of children by 'religious' stands out further as an abominable crime in our society because it is the betrayal of a sacred trust. It stirs visceral feelings of betrayal, anger and retribution. Along with the crime of abortion it is the holocaust of our time. Yet even in the cold analysis, investigation of and retribution for such abominable acts of abuse, the principles of natural justice should prevail. Otherwise there is a real danger the process of recovery and rehabilitation itself becomes an abuse.

It began on Friday 26 November 2009, the beginning of a catastrophic communications effort by the Dublin Archdiocese and the Communications Centre of the Bishops' Conference in response to the publication of the Murphy Report.

My working background is primarily forty years in the business of risk management and, more lately, combined with some understanding of communications. I served for one year, from September 2002 to October 2003, as Interim Director of Communications in the Dublin Archdiocese. During that time, and since, I met both survivors and perpetrators of clerical child sexual abuse. At that time I was also the Chairman of the National Safety Council (Road Safety). From 2000 to 2005 my primary interest was in reducing the number of road fatalities and serious injuries through policy development and implementation in that area. I continue to have an interest in that policy issue. That became a shared interest as I slowly developed some understanding of child abuse and abusers. With others I am involved in researching the related issue of suicide, based on applying a similar policy approach to road safety. My primary interest in all of these areas is in the prevention of harm now and in the future. My interest in the past is limited to what we can learn so we can make the future a better place. That is the essence of risk management.

Much of what I write below could be viewed as ill-informed, ill-judged or poorly researched. I have had limited time to do this. I take responsibility for these faults.

I have watched in astonishment and dismay as the events of the last ninety-four days have unfolded. On the morning of Sunday 20 December on the *Marion Finucane Show* on RTÉ 1, I replied to a question on the Murphy Report saying that what had happened in relation to the Report in the Dublin Archdiocese was a communications catastrophe. I spoke in support of Bishop Eamonn Walsh and Bishop Raymond Field. A print journalist later requested an explanation. This chapter seeks to supply that explanation.

In a crisis, there is a well established proven methodology for communicating – internally and externally – summarised as follows:

- Pull your team together with any specialist advisors as necessary.
- Determine exactly what the problem is.
- Establish the facts.
- Discuss and discern the course of action, urgent and important and continuous.
- Agree the actions and the responsibilities – who does what, by when and how do you confirm that these actions have been done?
- Agree the communications strategy.
- Agree who the spokesperson is.
- Agree, telling the truth as you know it with the facts as you have them, who the audience is (or audiences are) that you need to address – internal and external.

- Agree precisely the messages they need to hear, how they will hear them and when. Check when it's done that the message has got across in the way you intended.
- Repeat continuously, retelling as often as is required, to ensure that the messages are understood, truthfully and factually.
- Update and clarify as required.
- Identify and correct/rebut immediately any misunderstandings, misstatements/incorrect conclusions or mischievous statements by vested interests.
- Continue until the situation is recovered, and stabilised.
- Review and carry out any recovery/rehabilitation actions that are required.

That is an abbreviated version of crisis communications procedure.

Now apply this summarised procedure to the communications of the Dublin Archdiocese following the publication of the Murphy Report on 26 November and answer these questions:

- From the actions and words evidenced to date is the communication strategy of the Dublin Archdiocese clear?
- Is there evidence of clear internal and external communication?
- Are the messages communicated clearly, internally and externally, through the appropriate channels/media in an effective way?
- Is it clear that survivors of abuse, vocal and silent, are at the centre of the (care) message?
- Is it clear that the priests and lay faithful are important recipients of the message, that they are being informed honestly and consistently, and that there is a mechanism to take feedback, and that this feedback becomes part of the communication?
- Is it clear that the spokesperson and advisors have detailed knowledge of the cases and context and have the benefit of an objective editorial team who have honestly reviewed the report and documented clarifications, omissions, unintentional errors or misunderstandings or qualified conclusions to enable truth and fact in communication?
- Have errors of fact in media reporting been identified,

investigated and, where appropriate, rebutted and/or corrected and clarified? In this case there was abundant time, at least three years, to prepare this crisis communications procedure – was this done?

• And finally, has all of this been done in a way that reflects gospel values – these are the stated values of the organisation – that are central to the mission of the organisation?

The point is this. This entire context is about people, ordinary people, abused people, hurt people, wounded people, and their families and friends. The way the Report is being dealt with by the Archdiocese and Church administrators has itself become an abuse of people, their character and their reputation. This is not right. You do not right an injustice by committing another.

On 31 December 2009, the following series of questions was sent by email to Archbishop Martin and to the Priests' Council. Through their Chairman, the Council had become directly engaged in the communications process. The questions were copied to Cardinal Brady on 1 January 2010. The Archbishop acknowledged receipt and we met on 14 January at his request. He remains firm in his view that he is dealing with this crisis appropriately. The failure implied in the questions is not personal to Archbishop Martin. It is impossible not to feel compassion for the Archbishop in the position in which he finds himself – suddenly confronted by the imperative of dealing with a situation wholly outside his professional and pastoral competence. This does not detract from the argument that things should have been handled differently. Had this been done, it would at least have mitigated the difficulties in rebuilding trust in the Church in line with Christ's unequivocal demand to care for the little ones. Equally the apparent communications debacle – and the all too real sense of hurt, perhaps reflecting fragility in the exercise of authority – within the Episcopate and the Council of Priests, would also have been mitigated. The failure applies to the leaders of the all-island institutional Church. It is this institution, as an administrative function for the mission of the Church, which has failed. In particular, it has failed its priests, religious congregations and the lay faithful. In that institution there is accountability for those with authority and responsibility. The faith and mission of the Church, under the guidance of the Holy Spirit, thankfully, remains intact.

The following are the questions sent to Archbishop Martin, the Council of Priests and the Irish Bishops' Conference.

1. Preparation for the Murphy Report

- It is well known you wanted to prepare the Dublin Archdiocese, survivors/victims of abuse, priests and people in advance for the shocking impact of the Murphy Report. Why?
- You were concerned about the impact it would have. Why?
- What exactly were you concerned about?
- By all accounts the early preparatory meetings were vigorous and successful. After you completed these meetings, statements and pastoral visits, did you receive much reaction and/or responses? And if so how would you summarise this as to source and content?
- What part did your auxiliary bishops take in supporting you in this preparatory work?
- Did you discuss the responses and your experience with your 'Management Team' (the Diocesan Council) and with the Council of Priests?
- Following this preparatory work and feedback what were the key decisions in your crisis management plan to fix an Archdiocese in need of serious management change?
- Did you discuss these proposed changes with your management team and the Council of Priests?
- What were the key points of the crisis communication plan that you prepared following your preparatory work and feedback?

  For example, did you set up a team to provide you (and the Archdiocesan archive) with an objective analysis of the Murphy Report from a historical, social, legal (canon and civil law), risk management (prevent, contain, recover and rehabilitate), and communications perspective? Did you nominate team member(s) to research and prepare specific comments to comfort and reassure survivors/victims and recognise the sensitivity of their position? Did you nominate team members who could specialise and brief on the specifics of the individual cases, the history of the period known to those who participated, the key failures, the beginning of the writing and implementation of risk management procedures and the impact this had, the canon and civil law history and practice, the external professionals who were advisers during that time?

For example, did you nominate one or two people to deal with the internal and external communications aspects, bearing in mind that the people you would be addressing ranged from the survivors/victims, your fellow bishops, past and present auxiliary bishops, priests, congregations, lay volunteers and the lay faithful of your Church, and perpetrators of abuse? Did you nominate a support team who could prepare daily briefing summaries of the local and international media coverage so that 'truth and fact' clarifications could be issued quickly and accurately and rebuttal statements could be issued where necessary? Did you prepare a special section of the diocesan web site to ensure journalists (and others) would receive accurate information from the Archdiocese without having material reported second hand by a media that are more interested in sensation than truth and fact?

For example, did you prepare support for the known and accused perpetrators? Did you liaise with the Board for the Safeguarding of Children so as to share lessons learnt and improve prevention measures in the future? Did you seek data, research and advice on 'best practice' child protection risk management procedures from within and outside the Catholic Church and world wide?

In summary, did you prepare a crisis management and communications plan? If you were to prepare again, with the benefit of hindsight, would you have done anything differently to prepare for the publication of the Murphy Report? How would you describe the status of child protection in the Archdiocese today? How would you describe the morale of the priests and faithful of the Archdiocese today – five years into your mission, management and leadership?

2. Management of the Archdiocese

You are Archbishop of Dublin since 26 April 2004, having arrived here as Coadjutor in March 2003. That is a period of five years and seven months, nearly sixty-seven months or just over two thousand days. Why have you taken so long to implement serious management change in the administration of the Archdiocese – change, you say, that is very badly needed? Why did you not implement much sooner, these personnel changes you have now taken, and are proposing to take, some seventy months later? You have had power and authority since April 2004?

What precisely is the newly available information (on which you based your decisions for management changes) concerning overall administration of the Archdiocese but with particular emphasis on the administration activity of the auxiliary bishops in the context of clerical child sexual abuse that was not known to you from files and other recorded material on and since April 2004?

The Murphy Commission was announced in March 2006 and commenced work immediately. Final drafts were made available to you and other bishops for your review.

When did you decide on the consequent management and other personnel changes that were required? Whom did you consult? When? What did you tell the present and past auxiliary bishops? When did you first tell the present and past auxiliary bishops of your opinion, conclusions and decisions as indicated by you on *Prime Time* on 1 December 2009 and confirmed in subsequent days?

Do you believe that using *Prime Time* was an appropriate way to communicate this message for the first time to the survivors/victims of clerical child sexual abuse, to five past and present auxiliary bishops, to your priests and to your people? Do you believe that communicating through *Prime Time* in that way helped to ease the suffering of survivors and victims of clerical child sexual abuse? As you now reflect back on the confused and ambiguous comments made by you and your spokeswoman in statements and in media interviews since the publication of the Murphy Report, what do you think is the impact on the suffering of survivors and victims of clerical child sexual abuse? And particularly on those who choose to remain silent?

In retrospect, do you think you were helpful to your priests in fulfilling their mission to your people? Do you think you had any impact on the personal integrity of your serving auxiliary bishops, Eamonn Walsh and Raymond Field in fulfilling their work?

Taking one specific example, if your view of Bishop Eamonn Walsh was already formed on the day of the release of the Murphy Report, a view you later expressed on 1 December (*Prime Time* – four days later), and in your letter of 2 December and in your statement of 17 December (that spoke of 'collective responsibility'), and finally in your statement on 24 December (where you mentioned you had 'limited confidence' in Bishop Walsh), why then did you request Bishop Walsh to sit with you at your press conference on the report on 26 November and why did you nominate Bishop Walsh to act as your spokesperson to deal with the media the following day?

On 17 December, following the meeting of the Council of Priests, you released a statement saying this was the greatest crisis for the Dublin Archdiocese and you would not comment further until early in the New Year. You then left your Archdiocese in crisis. Did you appoint a spokesperson in your absence? And, if not, why did the Chairperson of the Council of Priests appear in the media speaking on your behalf, contradicting what you had said in your statement? Causing further confusion and ambiguity? And with no clarification from you or your media spokeswoman?

On Christmas Eve 2009, in a statement released to the media through your spokeswoman, you clarified an answer you gave to over three hundred priests at a meeting in City West on 12 December. Those who were present heard you respond that 'you had confidence in your auxiliaries'. Your recall is that you answered that 'you had confidence in their ministry but you could say nothing further till you had completed your review in early January 2010'. Your subsequent statement (24 December) clarified, from your perspective, why you could not have full confidence and why Bishop Walsh was wrong to imply that you had 'full confidence' in his personal letter to those in his deanery area with whom he had worked over the previous years. Bishop Walsh in fact in his letter only attributed to you the statement of confidence – a statement that is recalled by all of those asked who were at that City West meeting. Why was it necessary for you to clarify something that had never been claimed? When did you come to the conclusion that your confidence in your serving auxiliary bishops, for whom you are personally responsible, was limited only to the exercise of their ministry (24 December statement and briefing to journalists by your spokeswoman) and what exactly does this phrase mean?

Do you think it might have been reasonable for your two auxiliary bishops to rely on your confidence in them, given your working relationship with them since April 2004 and particularly over the last twelve months as you prepared for the publication of the Murphy Report? Why, over the last thirty days were serious errors of fact and misrepresentation not corrected by you or your communications spokeswoman?

Why do you now believe that Bishop Martin Drennan should resign? You included him in your *Prime Time* comments and in your letter to the five bishops. Are you aware of a perception you have created that in attempting to separate yourself and your career so comprehensively from the abominable behaviour of some priests of the past and the catastrophic consequences of that behaviour in this Archdiocese, that you may have added a further injustice to this appalling story? Do you have any awareness that in your efforts to put right the abominable injustice of clerical child sexual abuse you have added a further injustice in your treatment of your auxiliary bishops whom you have failed to support and in whom you have, in reality, expressed no confidence?

Errors of fact and misrepresentation
The chronology of events provided here from 26 November to 31 December 2009 and subsequently to 15 March is a matter of public record and can be accessed in the archive of *The Irish Times*, the *Irish Independent*, *The Examiner* and RTÉ.

A number of statements contrary to fact and truth have been established by and in the media and elsewhere due to the comprehensive failure of the communications offices of the Dublin

Archdiocese and the Irish Bishops' Conference to have in place a robust crisis communications procedure, including rebuttal, clarification and correction. That is a pity. It adds one injustice to another.

The most serious of these errors of fact and misrepresentation are:

• That there was widespread cover up among all priests – this was never adequately corrected and clarified;

• That there was 'collective responsibility' and, consequently, 'guilt by association' and 'general responsibility' among auxiliary bishops (and others), all concepts introduced by Archbishop Martin;

• That there was no learning curve, individually or collectively for the Archdiocese, in relation to clerical child sexual abuse and the issue of paedophile priests.

• Where are the voices of the silent professionals who worked for and with the Church over the last thirty and more years, lawyers, doctors, psychiatrists, councillors and therapists and a range of business people?

Where does the Cloyne Report (June 2008) leave the Conference of Bishops in relation to 'collective responsibility', 'guilt by association' and 'general responsibility'?

The only rational analysis to date of some of these issues was printed in the February 2010 edition of *The Furrow*.

Bishops Walsh and Field offered their resignations to Rome on 24 December 2009.

I am firm in my view that, while expressing and feeling all compassion for and empathy with victims of clerical child sexual abuse (and all those abused), a grave injustice has been done in the last three months to the lay faithful, good women, good men, good priests and good bishops. I have worked with Bishop Walsh and Bishop Field and so I single them out for that reason – because I can give testimony from personal experience. They have not asked for this, they are not aware of it, and in their humility they will not thank me for it. I sincerely hope that these comments do not add further to their burdens or those of others connected to this story of an abomination and criminality. This is a grave matter of injustice on which to remain silent is to concur.

The Future

As for the future? The Catholic Church in Ireland through the establishment of the Board for the Safeguarding of Children with John Morgan as Chairman and Ian Elliot as Chief Executive is probably now at the forefront of best practice policy in seeking to protect children from abuse. Implementation of the policy is urgently required, evidence-based implementation, in every diocese, parish and church activity. The State would do well to learn from this. In a few decades time there will be another report. Where then will the learning curve be? Where will collective responsibility be? Where will the cover-up be? Where will we be? What will we have done?

The beginnings of this next report have already started. Children today would be better served if we applied our energy and creativity towards rediscovering our Christian principles and values in order to prevent abuse in the future rather than concentrating on the diminishing value of blame for the past. The civil and criminal justice system is there to deal with the past. It works. We have learned from the past, thanks to Ryan and Murphy and the media. Prevention of abuse now and in the future requires a different mindset, attitude and very different actions.

CHAPTER FOURTEEN

Culture That Corrodes [1]

Donald Cozzens

How could Dublin's archbishops and bishops sleep at night? First the Ryan Report and now the Dublin Report, more formally known as the Report by the Commission of Investigation into the Catholic Archdiocese of Dublin, which found the leaders of the Dublin Church more concerned with secrecy, the avoidance of scandal, and the protection of the Church's reputation and resources than the pursuit of justice and the safety of their young.

Irish Catholics, still angry, dismayed and disillusioned by the Ryan Report, struggle to understand how high-ranking prelates could have behaved so irresponsibly. How could these shepherds of the Archdiocese of Dublin put the 'good of the Church' ahead of the welfare of vulnerable and innocent children being abused by Catholic priests? How indeed could they sleep at night?

I believe the Dublin prelates slept rather well – at least until the abuse scandals reached the tipping point beyond which their protest of innocence by way of ignorance could no longer be sustained. As the Dublin Report makes clear, Church authorities were guilty of much more than sleeping on the job. Is it within our own ability to comprehend the bishops' mindset, the mental manoeuvrings and the constrictions of conscience that resulted in such an abject failure in pastoral leadership and judgement?

What follows is an attempt at understanding the human and systemic factors that led intelligent, prayerful, well-educated men of the Church to behave in this way. They were not unique: the Dublin Report details a pattern of Church response to clergy sexual abuse that mirrors that of countless other archdioceses and dioceses throughout the Catholic world.

Why did these clerics have such an obsession with secrecy?

1. This chapter was previously published in *The Tablet* on 5 December 2009.

One explanation is the Church's insistence that its community of faith is a family – and for centuries a family that was a law unto itself. Consider for a moment how the head of a household might react if he discovered his adult son had sexually abused a young cousin. The cousin is underage and the son sadly admits to the criminal behaviour. The paterfamilias never even considers calling the police. His instinct is to protect the reputation of his family and to shield his son from prosecution and prison. And he thinks of himself as a decent man because he does what he believes is reasonable to make sure that there is no further abuse, perhaps even apologising to the young cousin. The abuse, of course, must remain a carefully guarded secret.

More and more priests wince these days when their bishop refers to them as his spiritual sons. But the language and parental image remain etched in the psyche of the ordained. Until recently, bishops regularly responded to reports of their priests abusing minors in the way described above – as a father might try to protect his household and contain the damage done by a wayward son, even when the son was guilty of a crime.

Damage control in these circumstances becomes the mindset of the bishop and his core advisers. The aim is to keep the abuse from the media so as not to cause scandal. A criminal investigation or a civil lawsuit might also threaten the financial stability of the diocese. And in these circumstances, the welfare of the victim is seldom the first concern of Church authorities.

This penchant for secrecy flows naturally out of the Church's feudal structure. Think of bishops as lords of the manor who until rather recently had discretionary control of the properties, personnel and financial resources of their dioceses – in truth, their benefices.

The expectations of today's Catholics are for accountability and openness from their bishops. But even in the post-conciliar era, many hierarchs insist that they are accountable only to the Pope. The bishop who behaves and thinks more like a feudal lord than a pastor and teacher considers secrecy a divine right.

Closely linked to the feudal structure of the Church is the centuries-old tradition of cloaking the office of bishop in the trappings of nobility. Bishops are not only lords of their manors, they are princes with all of the insignia, entitlements and exemptions associated with the noble houses of Europe. Furthermore, they are princes who carry the special mark of the Holy Spirit as successors to the apostles. It is their weighty responsibility to be men set apart in order to safeguard the faith and mission of the Church. From this perspective, it is easy to see why many bishops believe they know best what is to be made known to the faithful and what is to remain private – that is, secret – for the good of the Church.

Another factor that shapes the mindset of many bishops and influences how they have responded to the abuse scandals is the knotty issue of ambition. Ambition is as human a drive as the sexual instinct. In the Church, being overly ambitious is perceived as dreadfully bad form for a clergyman. A priest does not apply for a preferment nor is there a personnel board charged with processing priestly applications for the episcopacy. The same holds for a bishop who might have his eye on a more prestigious diocese or an appointment to the Vatican's curia.

Even bishops without an ambitious bone in their body know what the Holy See expects of them: good pastoral leadership, sound teaching of doctrine and adequate oversight of the patrimony of the diocese. On the negative side, of course, is the absence of scandal. Understandably, bishops want to avoid 'problems' that attract attention. When a bishop's desire to 'run a tight ship' is coupled with ambition for an appointment to a higher station, the instinct for secrecy and control tends to override all other concerns.

It's fair to assume the last thing a bishop wants to be held guilty of is idolatry. But I suspect that might be the real issue here. Like the rest of their fellow believers, archbishops and bishops must be alert to the idolatrous pull of status, power and money. For men raised to the station of bishop, however, idolatry's temptation is to make the protection and well-being of the institutional Church their ultimate aim. It is a deadly idolatry for it wears the mask of fidelity and loyalty to 'the good of the Church'.

These factors – secrecy, ambition, the remnant of feudal nobility, the temptation to idolatry – have shaped the mindset of not a few archbishops and bishops. The same factors can also be seen as fibres holding together what is now understood as clericalism, the nadir of the priesthood and episcopacy. Clericalism, like pornography, is difficult to define but we tend to know it when we encounter it. It is the sense of 'not being like the rest of men', a sense of preferment, exemption and privilege. It is a culture of privilege and betrays a marked absence of authenticity and integrity.

Clerical culture, the ecclesial world in which priests and bishops live, is a natural enough phenomenon. However, when it breeds clericalism, as it often does, it takes on a destructive force that compromises honest and effective leadership and ministry. Moreover, clericalism closes clerical eyes to the Church's ongoing need for renewal and reform. In this sense, clerical culture is a culture of secrecy and denial. Once drawn into its web, a cleric finds it is difficult to keep his priorities straight. He becomes like the storied medieval cardinal who bragged: 'I only lie in the best interests of the Church.'

There remain other, more fundamental questions to be addressed. Have the archbishops and bishops of Dublin asked why and how a significant number of their priests came to abuse teenagers and children? Their priests, after all, were educated in moral theology, sacred scripture and trained to be pastoral guides to their parishioners. Indeed, have the bishops of the world asked to what extent the systems, structures and culture of the clerical state contributed to the clergy abuse scandals? Such questions are judged dangerous precisely because they lead to neuralgic issues like mandated celibacy and conflicting theologies of the priesthood.

The Archdiocese of Dublin stands now in the dock of public scrutiny and judgement. But it certainly does not stand alone. I am unaware of any major diocese, anywhere, that has not had to cope with the tragedy of clergy abuse. Perhaps the Ryan and Dublin Reports will inspire the courage necessary to break through the cathedral-thick walls of secrecy and denial that have abetted and compounded unspeakable evils.

It's now Advent, the great season of hope. Perhaps the Catholics of Ireland will show the rest of the Catholic world how to face up to one of the saddest chapters in the history of the Church – for the good of the people of God, for the good of the children.

CHAPTER FIFTEEN

Quo Vadis? The Road to Rome

Garry O'Sullivan

The story of Peter fleeing Rome and meeting Jesus culminates in Peter's question to Jesus as to where is he going. Jesus replies: 'I am going to Rome to be crucified again.' Peter collects himself and his fear, turns on his heels and heads back to Rome. Thinking about the Irish bishops and communications around child sexual abuse, I've seen some of them fleeing out the back door of Maynooth in order to avoid being asked difficult questions. Child sexual abuse for the Irish bishops has been the path to crucifixion, but not their own martyrdom, though some easily take on the victim mantle. It is the crucifixion of an idea of priesthood, of Church, that was wrong and in some cases rotten. After the Murphy Report, the bishops didn't know where to go or what to do. It was pitiful. Eventually, they took the road to Rome to find answers at the feet of Peter's successor, who for twenty years oversaw Irish files of clerical abuse, indeed files from around the world. This is the timeline of how they got to Rome.

Boston and 'something rotten'
In 2002, when the clerical child abuse crisis rocked the Boston diocese and eventually forced resignation of Cardinal Bernard Law, a lay leader there perceptively said to a Boston journalist: 'We're only on page five of a five hundred-page Russian novel.' The same could have been said that year about the Irish abuse crisis, only at that time we were still on the preface of our Russian novel. The then Justice Minister Michael McDowell said on RTE's *Prime Time* programme that there was 'something very rotten at the heart of our society'. How right he was.

Eight years later we have uncovered more of the rottenness in the Murphy Report and we do not yet have the full story. There are two more chapters of the Murphy Report to be released later this year – it may well be that they have been released by the time that this book is being read. At least one of those chapters is expected, according to Church sources, to show extreme mishandling of an abuse case. The story is set to continue.

That this information is leaking out about those chapters sets the tone for a look at the overall communication of the Murphy Report by the Church authorities. After the publication of the report, Bishop Eamonn Walsh said one of the biggest faults of the Church structure as outlined in Murphy was that there was not proper communication. 'Everybody was in their own little cocoon, and if they had some information ... they kept it to themselves. As a result there was information but no co-ordination. Now that is very, very different.' While internal communications between departments may well now be better in Archbishop's House, overall communications are still woeful as the details below highlight. Looking back over a four-month period and the lead up to it should give a sense of perspective to this crisis and open up the communications strategy employed by the Church (cynics might like to quip 'if there was one', but we know there was) and how effective it was or what other forces were at play to undermine its effectiveness.

As far as we can ascertain, Bishop Eamonn Walsh was heading up a small team to help co-ordinate the response to the release of the Murphy Report, including Fr Joe Mullen, Chairman of the Priests' Council. This is not surprising, given Bishop Walsh's extensive experience of working in Ferns. Before the release of the report, it was becoming clear – those who were named in the report were sent draft copies of the parts of the report in which they were named – that Cardinal Connell would escape severe censure, but that the auxiliaries, especially Bishop Donal Murray of Limerick, would have questions to answer. It was said that Bishop Murray was prepared to defend himself and even had a press release ready for publication.

It is also important to note that we were well-prepared for a report that would be shocking. Some have said that we were prepared for the wrong report; everyone expected gory details about abuse. After all, we had already had the Ferns and Ryan Reports, not to mention the TV programmes that led to those reports. This would be different; it was the gross mismanagement by the hierarchy that people would react to rather than the facts of abuse, terrible abuse, that took place. It was the ongoing lack of management that would eventually mean the whole bishops' conference going to Rome for direction from the Pope and his key advisors.

28 November 2008: Archbishop Diarmuid Martin describes the scale of abuse by priests of the Dublin Diocese as 'staggering'. This letter – seen by *The Irish Catholic* newspaper – was sent by Archbishop Diarmuid Martin to priests in the Dublin archdiocese. In it, Dr Martin says that the fact that four hundred people have been abused by Dublin priests is staggering and the figure is most certainly not final. Dr Martin writes: 'We as priests are extremely upset and offended by what has happened through the actions of some.' The archbishop will host a number of meetings in early January 2009 to prepare priests for the fallout from the report of the Dublin Inquiry into abuse in the diocese, which is due to finish its work at the end of January. However we learn later that the report will be delayed.

16 June 2009: Archbishop of Dublin Diarmuid Martin's personal torment on reading files in the diocese's archives detailing clerical child sex abuse is reported. In one instance he said it prompted him to throw documents on the ground. Archbishop Martin recalls how: 'One weekend I decided to try and get through these documents. I came to the stage when I simply threw them on to the ground. I couldn't keep reading. This is reality. It can't be hidden and it shouldn't be hidden.'

He also says that co-operating with the Dublin commission often caused him sleepless nights. He would 'turn over at night and wonder whether I have done the right thing or made a mistake', he says.

Release of the report
15 October 2009: The High Court rules that the Murphy Commission's report into clerical child sexual abuse in the Dublin Diocese can be released except for Chapters 19 and 20, which contain material relating to three upcoming cases. The earliest of the three cases is expected to be heard in April 2010 and the High Court will reconsider the issue of publishing Chapter 19 in May 2010. The report considers how the Catholic

Church handled allegations of sexual abuse against a sample of forty six priests between 1 January 1975 and 30 April 2004.

19 November 2009: The High Court authorises the release of an edited version of the report, with references to three people removed.

26 November 2009: The Report is published. It consists of three volumes and cost €3.6 million to compile. The investigating commission identifies three hundred and twenty abused people between 1975 and 2004, and one hundred and twenty from May 2004. It states that the four archbishops, John Charles McQuaid, Dermot Ryan, Kevin McNamara, and Desmond Connell, who were serving during that time, handled complaints badly. One of the priests who admitted abuse stated he did so more than one hundred times. Another did so fortnightly for twenty five years. Another died in 2002, professing that he had done nothing wrong. Along with clergy, the Gardaí are accused in the report of covering up the scandal.

Archbishop Martin holds a press conference, flanked by Auxiliary Bishop Eamonn Walsh, to apologise, and has a letter to the priests and laity that will be read out at all Masses the following Sunday. 'The damage done to children abused by priests can never be undone,' he wrote. 'As Archbishop of Dublin and as Diarmuid Martin I offer to each and every survivor, my apology, my sorrow and my shame for what happened to them. I am aware however that no words of apology will ever be sufficient.'

27 November: Bishop Eamonn Walsh tells RTÉ that further investigations of dioceses would not serve any useful purpose: 'I would much prefer that we implemented the recommendations and put in place civil and legislative structures to live up to what we have found, but we could spend the next fifteen years going around the country when we'd be far better using our time, energy and money in consolidating our church-protection services, our school protection services and all of the legislation that will enable it.' Dr Walsh said the culture of 'don't ask, don't tell' and fear of scandal having primacy over the rights of children within the Catholic Church was 'dead and gone ... and if it is not, that person should be.'

Sunday 29 November: Bishop Donal Murray announces: 'As far as I am concerned the question of whether I should resign is a question of whether my presence here is a help or a hindrance to the diocese of Limerick'. Bishop Murray texts a message of support to Archbishop Martin.

30 November: Bishop Willie Walsh tells RTÉ's *Morning Ireland* that there is a gross misreading of the Dublin Report going on and recommends that if people are going to speak on that issue, they study very carefully the terms of the Dublin Report. He then admits that he hasn't read the report: 'I haven't had time to examine it in detail but I do know for a fact that some of the interpretation being put on that against Bishop Murray is a misreading of the report. I do know that from someone who has read in detail the report and I'm satisfied with that.' He later apologises on local radio.

1 December: Bishop Murray informs the Vicars General of his diocese of his decision to offer his resignation. He tells a journalist after the meeting that he will not be resigning.

Speaking on RTÉ's *Prime Time*, Archbishop Martin announces his intention to write to all auxiliary bishops named in the report as he is not satisfied with some of their responses so far. He says bishops should not look for support in their own diocese as the report refers specifically to the Archdiocese of Dublin. He says that he does not want to be sitting at meetings with people who he believes have not responded to very serious situations. He calls on bishops to make themselves accountable or resign. He complains that only two fellow bishops have offered him support since the publication of the Murphy Report.

2 December: Bishop Murray contacts the Papal Nuncio to arrange a meeting with the Congregation for Bishops in Rome. A spokesman for Bishop Murray confirms he received a letter for Archbishop Martin.

3 December: Theologian Vincent Twomey calls on all the bishops named in the report to resign. He says: 'At the very least, it would seem, all were guilty of negligence – some, such as Bishop Donal Murray of Limerick, whose behaviour was described as "inexcusable", more than others. But all were deemed guilty of inaction, of failing to listen to their conscience.' Fr Twomey would later pull back from this position and say that he did not think Bishop Drennan, a former colleague of his in Maynooth, should resign. Asked about his own time in Maynooth when Mícheál Ledwith was President, Dr Twomey says that 'we are all implicated'.

5 December: Cardinal Brady says Bishop Murray should do the right thing.

7 December: Bishop Murray meets with Cardinal Re in Rome who agrees to present the letter of resignation when he meets the Pope on 12 December.

December 9: The Irish Bishops Conference at its winter meeting issues a statement apologising to all abused and their families saying: 'We are deeply shocked by the scale and depravity of abuse as described in the Report. We are shamed by the extent to which child sexual abuse was covered up in the Archdiocese of Dublin and recognise that this indicates a culture that was widespread in the Church. The avoidance of scandal, the preservation of reputations of individuals and of the Church, took precedence over the safety and welfare of children. This should never have happened and must never be allowed to happen again. We humbly ask forgiveness.' The bishops go on to say that there was no place for 'mental reservation' in the Church when it came to dealing with abuse or 'covering up evil'. 'Charity, truthfulness, integrity and transparency must be the hallmark of all our communications.'

11 December: Cardinal Sean Brady and Archbishop Martin travel for a ninety-minute meeting with the Pope to brief him on Murphy. A pastoral letter is promised. Pope Benedict XVI says: 'The Holy See takes very seriously the central issues raised by the Report, including questions concerning the governance of local Church leaders with ultimate responsibility for the pastoral care of children. The Holy Father intends to address a Pastoral Letter to the faithful of Ireland in which he will clearly indicate the initiatives that are to be taken in response to the situation.'

'The Holy Father shares the outrage, betrayal and shame felt by so many of the faithful in Ireland, and he is united with them in prayer at this difficult time in the life of the Church. The Holy Father was deeply disturbed and distressed by its contents. He wishes once more to express his profound regret at the actions of some members of the clergy who have betrayed their solemn promises to God, as well as the trust placed in them by the victims and their families, and by society at large.'

At City West Hotel, Timothy Radcliffe speaks words of encouragement to Dublin's beleaguered priests; psychologist Tony Bates says psychologists are on a learning curve in relation to abuse. Archbishop Martin is asked from the floor if he supports his auxiliaries. He replies, according to some who were there, an unequivocal yes. His own spokesperson later said he only supported their ministry.

Sunday 13 December: Vincent Twomey reiterates his call for resignations and says the men concerned are 'causing continuing grave scandal'.

14 December: Bishop Murray is told by Cardinal Re that his resignation has been accepted and will be announced on 17 December. This is not made public.

16 December: *The Irish Catholic* exclusively reports that Bishop Donal Murray will resign at 11 am the following day. At his resignation in St John's Cathedral, Bishop Murray says he had asked the Pope to allow him to resign 'because I believed that my presence will create difficulties for some of the survivors who must have first place in our thoughts and prayers' and he apologises to victims who were abused. Quite pointedly, his statement expresses appreciation to Cardinal Brady for his support, with no mention of the Archbishop of Dublin.

17 December: Bishop Jim Moriarty of Kildare and Leighlin says on local radio that he 'should not resign for my partial involvement in the Fr Edmondus case but I want to add that no bishop can put his own position before the good of the Church'. He adds that he is prepared to go sooner if that is necessary and has discussions with Cardinal Brady and Archbishop Martin in that regard.

17 December: Cardinal Brady reacts to Dr Murray's resignation. Archbishop Martin reacts also and says, 'I am and will be meeting those in this diocese who are named in the report about the way this archdiocese is managed, about changes I want and that I consider vital for the future of the Archdiocese of Dublin'.

18 December: Bishop Drennan goes on RTÉ's *News at One* and says that he did not know of any crimes that he should have reported in the past, and that he was happy with the manner in which he dealt with things. On the same programme, Fr Joe Mullen, Chairman of the Dublin Council of Priests, says that the bishops named in the Murphy Report are good men with decent reputations, but he feels further resignations are inevitable. Fr Mullen admitted later that he wasn't speaking as Chairman of the Council of Priests, nor was he speaking on behalf of the Archbishop of Dublin.

23 December: Bishop Jim Moriarty announces that he has offered his resignation to the Pope and that 'from the time I became an Auxiliary Bishop, I should have challenged the prevailing culture'.

24 December: Bishops Walsh and Field approach Archbishop Martin and seek assurances of his backing. When these are not forthcoming, they both announce their resignations but fail to give a reason for same.

29 December: The One in Four group call on Bishop Drennan to do the 'honourable thing' and resign.

The reaction to Murphy continues into January, with a call for 'a change of heart' by Fr Dermot Lane, writing in *The Furrow*. Stressing that any thoughts of 'business as usual' were misplaced, he adds that 'cosmetic changes' would not suffice to address the current crisis. He argues that any reform must be 'a change of heart with a new programme of reform [and] restructuring must result in new forms of governance and accountability'.

21 January 2010: *The Irish Catholic* exclusively reveals that the Pope has summoned the Irish bishops to Rome to discuss the fall-out from Murphy. The two-day meeting is scheduled for 15-16 February and set to include senior Vatican advisors. In the same issue of the newspaper, Monsignor Alex Stenson dismisses any suggestion that he, as Chancellor to three archbishops, should resign. He offers his own oversight of events in Dublin in a feature-length article entitled 'Putting the record Straight'.

28 January: *The Irish Catholic* is able to report exclusively on reaction to Murphy from within the ranks of the clergy as letters circulated by Bishop Dermot O'Mahony come to light. In one, to members of the Council of Priests, retired auxiliary Bishop O'Mahony outlines criticisms he made of Archbishop Martin's own response to the publication of Murphy, during a 30 November 2009 meeting of the Diocesan Council. He reveals he said to Dr Martin: 'Your criticism was unfair. You were out of the diocese for thirty one years and had no idea how traumatic it was for those of us who had to deal with the allegations without protocols or guidelines or experience in the matter of child sexual abuse.'

Bishop O'Mahony was especially upset at his treatment by Dr Martin, given that he issued his own letter of remorse for his part in the elements reported by Murphy on 27 October, and was later required by Dr Martin (in a letter of 2 December) to withdraw from Confirmations and to end his association with the Irish Handicapped Children's Pilgrimage to Lourdes. Notably, Dr Martin wrote: 'You did not express any public clarification or remorse or apology. It appears that you underestimate the degree of dismay and anger that people feel about the Commission's references to you.'

Ahead of the Rome meeting, Cardinal Brady rules out any role for lay representatives.

4 February: Further criticisms of Archbishop Martin emerge in the minutes of a priests' meeting held on 18 January. Recording that priests were 'dumbfounded' at Dr Martin's letter to Bishop O'Mahony, the minutes also complain of a lack of compassion shown for auxiliaries who were 'hung out to dry'. There was a general feeling that Dr Martin is a source of division among priests who are 'no longer content to be puppets of the diocese'.

A letter written by Bishop Eamonn Walsh a week before announcing his intention to resign comes to light also. It outlines a defence of his career, blaming bad communications which 'led to long-term disastrous consequences'.

8 February: At a meeting with representatives of the bishops at Maynooth, survivors of institutional abuse hand over a sealed letter to be conveyed to Pope Benedict. In parallel, survivors of clerical abuse co-sign an open letter in which they urge the Pope to accept the resignations of bishops implicated in Murphy and to move on the one bishop remaining at the head of his diocese, Bishop Martin Drennan of Galway.

15 February: On the eve of the Rome meeting, Fr Harry Bohan warns that another apology will not be enough to deal with the crisis in the Irish Church, and that only total reformation will address the issue. Fr Bohan wrote: 'We have to change or die' and move 'from a clerical culture ... dominated by clergy and clerically minded lay-people. Nothing short of total reform-ation of structures and leadership will suffice. We must return to first beginnings'. This, he added, 'is a pivotal moment in the life of our Church'.

Conclusion

This is not an exhaustive list of the events which happened but it gives a flavour of the pace of how events unfolded and how a diocese which seemed to be prepared for the Report apparently got overtaken by the tsunami of anger that followed. Bishop Eamonn Walsh was at the press conference responding to the Murphy report and on national radio. A short time afterwards he was fighting for his survival.

Archbishop Martin was the lone voice calling for account-ability, but he too, by riding on the angry tidal wave of opinion, seemed to lose the backing of his brother bishops and indeed of many of his priests. It was said that nobody disagreed with where he was trying to bring the Church, and indeed the bishops' state-ment in December was surprising to many in its acknowledge-ment of a culture that was widespread in the Church, but they did privately disagree with the way he was trying to do it.

What will happen now post-Rome and the negative fall-out? Certainly the communications were all wrong, but the bishops do seem to have a plan, a process. It is not all negative; we have to find the hand of God in this. After all, the light is being shone into the darkness.

I started by saying that this was like a Russian novel, so as one famous Russian novelist once said: 'The pages are still blank, but there is a miraculous feeling of the words being there, written in invisible ink and clamouring to become visible'.

For Peter, the journey back to Rome was the end of a painful quest. He was afraid, lacking in courage, in understanding of Jesus' will. He came to comprehend that in order to ascend we sometimes have to descend, like Christ, into pain and humili-ation.

CHAPTER SIXTEEN

Disturbing the Faithful:
Aspects of Catholic Culture Under Review

Louise Fuller

The following is an excerpt from a letter recorded in the *Irish Catholic Directory* on 10 April 1951:

> At a time when so many of the workers of various countries have fallen prey to false theories and ideologies that are in direct contrast to the Christian religion, it was a source of particular gratification to His Holiness to receive this further proof of the devoted attachment of the workers of Ireland to the Vicar of Christ, and to their fidelity to the Catholic Faith, which is their nation's most precious heritage.[1]

This letter was received by the Secretary of the Congress of Irish Unions, from Monsignor Montini, substitute Papal Secretary of State and future Pope Paul VI, acknowledging the address of homage and chasuble presented to Pope Pius XII during the Holy Year 1950, in the name of the workers of Ireland. It gives a sense of the impression of Ireland held in Rome in the early 1950s. Irish prelates felt very lucky and had good reason to be proud, as they were the envy of many of their European counterparts. Sixty years later, Pope Benedict XVI has decided to issue a special pastoral letter to the Catholics of Ireland and there is nothing gratifying about the context in which this letter is to be sent. Rather have recent reports and investigations revealed a very dark side to Irish Catholicism. What is interesting also is that while the pastoral letter will be addressed to all Catholics, lay and clerical, it is the actions of clergy, bishops and religious which have prompted the Pope's letter, and they may in due course lead to radical changes in the structures of governance in the Irish Church.

The authority of the once all-powerful Catholic Church in

1. *Irish Catholic Directory*, 1952 (1 May 1951), pp 652-3.

Ireland has gradually been eroded since the 1950s. There have been several landmarks on the way but, in the eyes of many observers, what has driven the final nail in the coffin is the litany of scandals that have wracked the Church more or less since the story of Bishop Eamonn Casey broke in May 1992. The narrative of Irish Catholicism changed profoundly from that time and the last word is not yet written. Recent chapters have been less than edifying, revealing details of clerical child sexual abuse in the diocese of Ferns,[2] physical, emotional and sexual abuse which took place in industrial schools as published in the Ryan Report in May 2009[3] and details of clerical child sexual abuse in the Dublin Archdiocese from 1975-2004, as published in the Murphy Report.[4] The diocese of Cloyne[5] is now to be investigated by the Murphy Commission and there may be more diocesan investigations to follow.

It is not the business of the historian to make prognostications about the possible implications of what has happened for the future of the Catholic Church in Ireland. Many churchmen and lay people are wrestling with the question of how it could come to this. What the historian can do is to take the long view of how the Church has developed in Irish society, and to pose questions in the light of the findings of these reports – which may yield up insights into the situation and predicament of the Church in Irish society today. This in turn may point to implications and possible future directions. These reports dealt with the physical, psychological and sexual abuse of children by nuns, priests and brothers. Abuse of any kind is profoundly upsetting because it is an assault on the dignity of another human being – the damage lasts a lifetime and has a ripple effect in all areas of a person's life and relationships. It is even more upsetting, if it is inflicted by a person or persons who are in a caring role and in situations which should constitute a safe

2. *The Ferns Report* (Dublin: The Stationery Office, 2005).
3. *Report of the Commission to Inquire into Child Abuse* (Ryan Report hereafter), (Dublin: The Stationery Office, 2009).
4. *Commission of Investigation Report into the Catholic Archdiocese of Dublin* (Murphy Report hereafter), (Dublin: The Stationery Office, 2009).
5. This is arising from the findings of a report, issued by the National Safeguarding Board for Children in the Catholic Church, in June 2008. The report found that Catholic Church authorities in the diocese of Cloyne had not responded properly to abuse allegations.

haven for children, as in the case of parents in the home, or relatives or Church personnel, in whom one should be able to place
one's trust. It is a topic which most people find extremely upsetting, to say the least.

How then was it that those in authority in the Church failed
to take responsibility and hand perpetrators up to justice? It
would appear that their sense of wrongdoing was profoundly
different from that of the general public. The Murphy Report
states categorically that 'all the archbishops and many of the auxiliary bishops in the period covered by the Commission handled
child sexual abuse complaints badly'.[6] While a few priests were
courageous and brought complaints to the attention of their
superiors, 'the vast majority simply chose to turn a blind eye'.[7]
When complaints came to the notice of the authorities, they
shielded the perpetrators and moved them on to new parishes
where they could re-offend. The excuse was made that in the
past, the nature of paedophilia was not fully understood, that it
was seen as a psychological disorder and that if somebody got
treatment, they could be rehabilitated. It was claimed that the
recidivist nature of this phenomenon was not fully known or
understood. But all such excuses were rejected by the Commission. It refused to accept pleas of ignorance. It pointed to 'a
two thousand year history of Biblical, Papal and Holy See statements showing awareness of clerical child sex abuse',[8] the first
denunciation dating from 153 AD.[9] The Commission cited the
Vatican's 1922 *Crimen Solicitationis* document, updated in 1962,
which addressed clerical child sexual abuse.[10]

A further instruction came from the Vatican in May 2001,
which directed the bishops to refer directly to the Congregation
for the Doctrine of the Faith (CDF) in Rome 'all allegations of
child sexual abuse, which have reached the threshold of "a sem-
blance of truth".'[11] The Commission's report also pointed to the

6. Murphy Report, p 10.
7. Ibid., p 7.
8. Ibid., p 5.
9. Ibid.
10. Ibid., p 61.
11.Ibid., p 64. See translation of *Sacramentorum Sanctitatis Tutela* on
http://www.opusbonosacerdotii.org/sacramentorum_sanctitatis_tute
la_english1.htm

inconsistency between claims that officials of the archdiocese were 'on a learning curve', given that inquiries were first made 'about insurance cover for compensation claims in the mid 1980s' and the fact that 'such cover was put in place in 1987'.[12] When it came to matters of finance, the Church clearly understood that claims for damages and compensation could potentially have enormous consequences for Church revenues.

The problem about child abuse is that it generates such an understandably extreme reaction in people, that there is little inclination to examine the broader picture. Almost daily, as we listen to the news, we are forced to confront the fact that human nature can be warped and we have to face the fact that, sadly, there will always be violence, evil and crime. That is not to suggest that one can be complacent. A distinction must be drawn between the perpetrators of these crimes and those who were in positions of authority over them. Perpetrators must be brought to justice and the question must be posed, given the enormity of their crimes, how was it that those in authority failed to live up to their responsibilities? These are people who preach the gospel ideal of love of God and one's neighbour. They laid down the rules of morality for the laity and set very high standards for them, particularly in the area of sexual morality. In fact, there are those who claim that, in some ways, sexual sin was the only sin ever really emphasised in the Irish Church to the point of obsessiveness. Against this background, the Church authorities' lack of response to infringements in this area seems totally inconsistent. It also raises the question, as to whether the very narrow and rigid teaching on sexual morality, preoccupied as it was with occasions of sin and constant warnings about impure thoughts and actions, have, in some cases, pre-empted certain proclivities in some people.

What many victims have stated is that the lack of understanding, aggressive approach and downright dishonesty of some in authority towards them, when they made allegations against abusers, was even harder to take than the abuse itself. This was borne out by the Murphy Report, which was very forthright in describing the attitude to individual complainants

---

12. Murphy Report, p 6.

as 'overbearing and in some cases underhand'.[13] The Commission, on the other hand, was impressed by the way complainants and their families behaved, pointing out that they 'frequently behaved in a much more Christian and charitable way than the Church authorities did'.[14] The old catechism taught that a lie was always sinful,[15] but it appeared that there were different rules for the clerical caste than for lay Catholics. The Report outlined the Church concept of 'mental reservation', which 'permits a churchman knowingly to convey a misleading impression to another person without being guilty of lying'.[16] For those familiar with pre-Vatican II moral theology, as exemplified in the 'Notes and Queries' section of the *Irish Ecclesiastical Record*, there is nothing new here. Essentially it is the casuistic method – a legalistic approach to moral theology. Such was the emphasis on adhering to the letter of the law, that moral theologians in this tradition essentially devised clever ways of getting around the law and not committing sin.[17] One would have thought that this kind of thinking was laid to rest with the 'new' theology of Vatican II. This kind of *mentalité*, which facilitated clerics in dealing with people in a dishonest way, has understandably occasioned both disillusionment and deep cynicism. One journalist, commenting on this phenomenon of 'mental reservation', observed that at times while reading the report, she felt that 'some of the senior clerics inhabited a kind of weird parallel universe that apparently made sense to them', but was 'utterly incomprehensible to anyone outside it'.[18]

Whatever compassion was shown seems to have been only towards clerics, in order to protect their good name and status in the Church. The priority was to prevent scandal for the

---

13. Ibid., p 10.
14. Ibid., p 27.
15. *Catechism of Catholic Doctrine*, (Dublin: M.H. Gill and Sons Ltd, 1951), no 264, p 64.
16. Murphy Report, pp 643-4. See also Dominic M. Prümmer OP, *Handbook of Moral Theology* translated from Latin by Rev Gerald W. Shelton (Cork: The Mercier Press, 1956), pp 134-5.
17. See Louise Fuller, *Irish Catholicism since 1950: the Undoing of a Culture* (Dublin: Gill and Macmillan, 2002), pp 32-6.
18. See Breda O'Brien, 'Opinion and Analysis', in *The Irish Times*, 28 November 2009.

Church as an institution, at all cost – and, ironically, the cost has proved much higher as a result. A big preoccupation for the Church has always been that the faithful must not be 'disturbed'. It was a Church and religion of certainties and it resulted in bishops, priests and religious being seen as having all the answers and, as a result, being placed on a very high pedestal, and it was seen as a catastrophe if they were perceived to have faults. Catechetics teaching did not lend itself to people understanding the fact that there were/are grey areas in theology. People were encouraged in their simple, child-like faith – but there were those even in the fifties who questioned this and saw its inadequacy.[19]

On the day the Murphy Report was published, Dermot Ahern, Minister for Justice, inadvertently touched on this, when he pointed out the necessity of reflecting on how a situation came about whereby a culture of deference to the Catholic Church, in some cases, had the effect of placing the behaviour of certain clergy beyond the reach of the law.[20] He emphasised the fact that Ireland is a republic. It was interesting that he should make the point, and not without irony. From the time of independence one of the foremost characteristics of the Irish republic was the close relationship that developed between Church and State. That critical attribute of republicanism, which emphasised the State's independence from the Church and led to the separation of Church and State in France in 1905,[21] did not hold sway in the Irish republican tradition. Catholic precepts were upheld in legislation and in the 1937 Constitution, and politicians did not see their way to challenging the Church, even in matters that rightly concerned them. Legislative and constitutional support for the Catholic ethos has gradually been dismantled over the past several decades,[22] but the Church is still a considerable power-broker in the areas of health and education. Church per-

19. See Fuller, *Irish Catholicism*, pp 82-3.
20. *The Irish Times*, 27 November 2009, p 9.
21. See Louise Fuller, 'The French Catholic Experience: Irish Connections and Disconnections', in Eamon Maher, Eugene O'Brien and Grace Neville (eds), *Reinventing Ireland through a French Prism* (Frankfurt am Main: Peter Lang, 2007), p 109.
22. See Fuller, *Irish Catholicism*, pp 239-50.

sonnel are involved in people's lives on the happiest and saddest of occasions. People rely on them when they are at their most
vulnerable, so this gives them enormous cachet, which ideally
should breed humility and a sense of privilege, but can, and in
some cases obviously does, breed a kind of superiority and
arrogance, whereby one might feel oneself to be above the law.
What these reports indicate is that a legacy of deference towards
the Church still prevails, which has prevented civilian authorities in many cases from carrying out their lawful duties. The
findings of recent reports have led to calls for the Church to relinquish its control at primary education level.[23]

When he was setting up the Church, Jesus addressed the following words to Peter: '... Thou art Peter; and upon this rock I
will build my church, and the gates of hell shall not prevail
against it. And I will give to thee the keys of the kingdom of
heaven.'[24] Churchmen can take refuge and consolation in these
words from scripture, but one wonders what the shape of his
Church would be. It does seem unlikely, based on the gospel
story, that it would resemble the institution as we know it today.
The fall-out from these scandals has been such that it must force
the Church to take stock. When one looks at many aspects of the
Church as it is today – the pomp and ceremony, what can only
be called the second-class status of women, the declining number of vocations – there is much to be concerned about and yet
there has been little engagement with such central issues of concern on the part of influential Church personnel.[25] Perhaps it
takes something catastrophic, which threatens to bring the edifice
crashing down, to get the establishment to be proactive about
renewal. The Vatican Council, almost fifty years ago, defined
the Church as the 'people of God'[26] and authority in the Church

23. A recent *Irish Times*/Ipsos MRBI opinion poll revealed that 61% of
the sample questioned expressed the opinion that the Catholic Church
should relinquish its control over education at primary school level. See
The Irish Times, 25 January 2010.
24. New Testament, Matthew 16:18-19.
25. See Tony Flannery, 'The Challenge Facing the Irish Church', in
Doctrine and Life, vol 59, no 2 (February 2009), pp 49-53.
26. *Dogmatic Constitution on the Church*, 21 November 1964, in Walter M.
Abbott (ed), *The Documents of Vatican II* (London, Dublin: Geoffrey
Chapman, 1966), Chap 2, p 24.

was defined as 'service'.[27] This was a very humble, participatory vision of Church. But the ideals laid down at Vatican II have not been realised in practice.

Had there been equal sharing of power with lay members of the Church, there may have been more questioning and this would have been far healthier for the Church's development. Of course, all of these events have led to considerable *Schadenfreude* in certain quarters. A once powerful institution has been brought to its knees and humbled in spite of itself. This is particularly the case for those who took the strictures of the Church to heart in the past and who tried earnestly to live by them, and are now, understandably, very disillusioned. Likewise those who did not quite manage to live up to the very high standards that the Church set for them, now see that some representatives of that institution were not practising what they preached, and this has led to understandable cynicism. The danger of a climate of revenge-seeking is that it can generate more heat than light. This does not increase understanding. Anger must be tempered with reflection. It is salutary to note that those who actually experience evil are often the least dogmatic in relation to it. Solzhenitsyn, who experienced the Siberian labour camps, saw the line between good and evil in people as very tenuous. When we hear stories of heroic people who sacrificed their lives to harbour others in Nazi Germany, we all like to think that, were we in that situation, we would do the right and virtuous thing – but there is no way to be sure. This is, in no way, to absolve those in authority from their responsibilities, merely to point out that they are only human, that the world is a messy place and that bad things happen to good and bad people.

Although the Church is a spiritual institution, it has a very significant investment and role in secular society. But in some ways it operates in a kind of parallel universe which transcends the ordinary temporal sphere. Unlike other organisations, it is not normally subject to external investigations or quality reviews.[28] It is interesting then that the Commission examined and

---

27. Ibid., Chap 3, para 18, 37.
28. It is well to note here, however, that investigatory and regulatory systems in the secular sphere have by no means lived up to their promise.

commented on the management of the archdiocese, pointing out that 'as an organisation operating within society, it seems to the Commission that the Church ought to have some regard to secular requirements in its choice of a leader ... Appointments to positions as archbishops and bishops seem to have been made primarily on the basis of doctrinal orthodoxy. Management ability does not seem to have been a relevant criterion'.[29] The Church, of course, makes no apologies for this, often pointing out that it has never claimed to be a democratic institution, but in this day and age, perhaps it can no longer be complacent about being an autocracy. When one considers battles in the past revolving around the issue of the independence of the Church in its choice of bishops, it is interesting to observe a State Commission presuming to comment critically on the criteria for the appointment of bishops. It is even more interesting, because this has been one of the burning issues for clergy for many years. Many priest commentators have pointed to the fact that the idea of a constitutional process is a charade, noting that Rome decides on the suitability of a candidate on the basis of his orthodoxy on certain key issues, with little or no account taken of the opinions of the local clergy.[30]

In 1994, Father Joe Dunn gave his reflections on how bishops were appointed in his book *No Lions in the Hierarchy*.[31] As first Director of the Catholic Communications Institute, established in 1969, he worked closely with the bishops for fourteen years and 'got to know the culture'.[32] In his experience, 'laity and priests have no say .... Everything is decided for them between Rome and (sometimes) the local hierarchy, in total secrecy'.[33] He also pointed out that 'Rome places too much emphasis on loyalty to the Holy See, to the detriment of other important leadership qualities'.[34] Indeed the very title of his book has an uncannily ironic ring to it today, in light of the failure of highly intelligent,

---

29. Murphy Report, pp 14-15.
30. See Brendan Hoban, 'A Time for Courage', in *The Furrow*, vol 60, no 6 (June 2009), pp 344-5.
31. Joseph Dunn, *No Lions in the Hierarchy: An Anthology of Sorts* (Dublin: The Columba Press, 1994), pp 26-48.
32. Ibid., p 27.
33. Ibid., p 47.
34. Ibid., p 48. In this general regard, see also 'A Bishop for Cork: new

well-educated, well-qualified churchmen to challenge the prevailing culture of the Church. It seems to have been a culture
that 'emasculated' otherwise competent, and let it be said, decent people and prevented them from following the law. There
has been much discussion in recent years in Ireland of how difficult it is for insiders to challenge the prevailing culture of an
organisation – from the banking profession, to the medical profession, to the State employment and training agency, FÁS.
Nonetheless, the point will be made, that one expects more from
Church personnel. The Ryan Report gives an insight into the
culture of religious life and deals with the impact that the vows
taken by the Mercy Sisters may have had on the institutional
care they provided.[35] The Murphy Report has pointed to the
culture of secrecy which prevented archbishops and bishops
from reporting complaints to the Gardaí prior to 1996.[36] It pointed
to the fact that 'a similar "culture of secrecy" was identified by
the Attorney General for Massachusetts in his report on child
sexual abuse in the Boston Archdiocese.'[37] As in the case of
Dublin, secrecy 'protected the institution at the expense of children'.[38] Bishop Jim Moriarty of Kildare and Leighlin and formerly
Auxiliary Bishop in Dublin, in his statement announcing his resignation in the aftermath of publication of the report, acknowledged 'the fact that the system of management and communications was seriously flawed' and went on to add: 'However, with
the benefit of hindsight, I accept that, from the time I became an
Auxiliary Bishop, I should have challenged the prevailing cult
ure'.[39] These reports are forensic examinations of the culture
within Catholic institutions and the Church is not accustomed
to such investigations.

departure or same old story', in *Céide: A Review from the Margins*, vol 1,
no 1 (September-October, 1997), pp 10-11. See also Thomas J. Reese,
Inside the Vatican: The Politics and Organisation of the Catholic Church
(Cambridge, London: 1996), p 236. For an account of the selection
process and appointment of bishops, see pp 234-42.
35. See Ryan Report, Vol II, pp 242-3.
36. Murphy Report, pp 8-9.
37. Ibid., p 8.
38. Ibid.
39. See statement 23 December 2009, Kildare and Leighlin diocesan
website http://www.kandle.ie/2009/12/23/moriarty-resignation/

In any exploration of Catholicism, it is important to remember that the local Church is a microcosm of the Church universal, based in Rome. Historically, Rome is the headquarters of the Catholic Church – it is where the rules are set out and policies are enunciated. Yet when the Commission wrote to the Congregation for the Doctrine of the Faith and to the Nuncio, the Vatican's representative in Ireland, for documentation which might be relevant to their investigation, they received no reply. Responding to charges that neither his office, nor Rome, had responded to queries from the Commission, the Nuncio, Archbishop Giuseppe Leanza pointed out that, given that the period covered by the report was from 1975 to 2004, and that he had only arrived in Ireland the previous year, he was not in a position to comment, that it was a matter for the archbishop of Dublin.[40] Likewise the Vatican spokesman, Fr Federico Lombardi, defended Rome's lack of response, stating that 'in all cases like this, it is not appropriate for Rome to comment, rather that is for the local bishop'.[41] But in both cases their excuses rang hollow. A letter writer to *The Irish Times* captured the mood of many, when he caustically remarked: 'Are we to believe that Irish bishops are a law onto themselves and take no instruction from the Vatican?'[42] It was understandable that many should feel that Rome wants it both ways. The Nuncio was requested to attend a meeting with Micheál Martin, Minister for Foreign Affairs, at Iveagh House 'to discuss issues surrounding the report', including 'the commission's findings as well as the issue of the co-operation of the nuncio and the Holy See with the commission'.[43] The symbolism was not lost on long-term observers of Church-State relations in Ireland. In the not too distant past, ministers would have been summoned to the bishop's palace.

It is important to bear in mind that not all priests and religious were involved in abuse or paedophilia. And it is important to recognise that there were systems failures at all levels. The

---

40. See *The Irish Times*, 1 December, p 7.
41. Quoted by Paddy Agnew, *Irish Times* correspondent in Rome, in *The Irish Times*, 27 November 2009. Similarly Irish bishops were loathe to comment on abuse issues in fellow bishops' dioceses.
42. *The Irish Times*, 1 December 2009, p 15.
43. Quoted in *The Irish Times*, 4 December 2009.

Murphy Report has highlighted the shortcomings of the State authorities and the Gardaí.[44] The Ryan Report criticised the deferential and submissive attitude of the Department of Education towards the Congregations as having 'compromised its ability to carry out its statutory duty of inspection and monitoring of the schools'.[45] The Ferns Report, pointing to the inadequacy of the approach of the Gardaí, observed that it may have been due to 'reluctance on the part of members of An Garda Síochána to investigate allegations of wrongdoing by members of the Catholic clergy'.[46] It concluded that 'the Church authorities, the medical profession and society generally failed to appreciate the horrendous damage which the sexual abuse of children can and does cause'.[47] And it is very important to recognise, and acknowledge, that the broader Irish society is not blameless. Many people knew that the treatment of children in industrial schools was not what it should be, and were happy enough to turn a blind eye.

There is no doubting the fact that aspects of the culture of Irish Catholicism, much vaunted in the 1950s, on investigation have been called into question and seen to be deeply flawed. The Ferns, Ryan and Murphy reports leave the Church with some very uncomfortable questions in relation to authority, communication, clerical culture, celibacy, sexuality, its attitudes towards the laity and the formation that priests and nuns received in the past.[48] In the pre-Vatican II era, much of the emphasis in Irish Catholicism was on sinfulness, the need for self-mortification, fear of the Lord and there was the constant threat of punishment and eternal damnation in the event of wrongdoing. Human nature was represented as inherently flawed since the original sin of Adam and Eve. The aim of the religious in all of

44. See Murphy Report, pp 23-6
45. Ryan Report, Executive Summary, Conclusions, p 11.
46. Ferns Report, Executive Summary, p ii.
47. Ibid., p iii.
48. See Bishop Willie Walsh, 'Reflecting on the Ryan Report', in *The Furrow*, vol 60, no 11 (November 2009), pp 579-587 In this article, Bishop Walsh writing as a cleric, who has come through the system at every level, explores aspects of Catholic culture which may have contributed to the tragic outcomes outlined in the Ryan Report, but which could equally apply to the other reports, as cited here.

170

his or her endeavours was to rise above human nature. The ethos was intended to subdue the person, to make him or her conform. For many it was not the kind of context which lent itself to fulfilment, or personal enrichment. This is not to say that the *mentalité* of Catholicism was entirely negative, just to point out that certain values, as mediated to some people and in turn mediated by them, did not always enhance lives, but rather impoverished them. While, in theory, the Catholic Church underwent profound and fundamental change in all aspects of its theology at the time of the Vatican Council, many of the findings in these reports relate to a period long after the Council and these changes do not appear to have found their way into Church practice. While the recent reports are concerned with the issue of abuse on many levels, the implications for the Church go far beyond the abuse issue. They raise deep and fundamental questions about Catholic culture, questions which are not confined to Ireland. They concern issues deeply embedded in Catholic history and theology. The present writer[49] and many others have highlighted this before the Ferns, Ryan and Murphy reports were published. At the beginning of the third millennium, there is much for the local and universal Church to ponder.

49. Fuller, *Irish Catholicism*, pp 267-8.

Editors and Contributors

Editors

JOHN LITTLETON, a priest of the Diocese of Cashel and Emly, is Head of Distance Education at The Priory Institute, Tallaght, Dublin. He is a chartered manager, a Fellow of the Institute of Leadership and Management and a Fellow of the Chartered Institute of Personnel and Development, with an interest in applying organisational development techniques to the changing of Church structures. He served for six years (2001-2007) as President of the National Conference of Priests of Ireland. His recent publications include *What Being Catholic Means to Me* (2009), co-edited with Eamon Maher, and *Journeying through the Year of Luke: Reflections on the Gospel* (2009).

EAMON MAHER is Director of the National Centre for Franco-Irish Studies in IT Tallaght, where he also lectures in Humanities. This is the fourth co-edited book dealing with the topic of contemporary Irish Catholicism on which he has worked. He is the editor of the successful *Reimagining Ireland* series with Peter Lang Oxford. He is currently writing a second monograph on John McGahern entitled *'The Church and its Spire': John McGahern and the Catholic Question*, which will be published later this year by The Columba Press.

Contributors

RICHARD CLARKE has been the Bishop of Meath and Kildare since 1996. He is the chair of the Church of Ireland's Commission for Christian Unity and Dialogue, and is also the current President of the Irish Council of Churches. Now widowed, he is the father of a son and a daughter, both medical doctors. In recent years he has authored two books, *And Is It True?* (2000) and *A Whisper of God* (2006).

MARIE COLLINS has been a vocal spokesperson for the survivors of clerical sexual abuse in the Dublin Archdiocese for many years. She herself was subjected to this abuse while a patient in Crumlin children's hospital. Along with other victims, she lobbied the government for the setting up of the Murphy Commission. Marie has been married for thirty-four years and has one son.

EAMONN CONWAY is a priest of the Tuam Diocese and Professor of Theology at Mary Immaculate College, University of Limerick. He co-edited, with E. Duffy and A. Shields, *Child Sexual Abuse and the Catholic Church – Towards a Pastoral Response* (1999). Since then he has published several papers on the subject in Ireland, the USA and Germany.

DONALD COZZENS, a priest, writer and lecturer, teaches in the Religious Studies Department at John Carroll University, Cleveland, Ohio. He has written *The Changing Face of the Priesthood* (2000), *Sacred Silence: Denial and the Crisis in the Church* (2002), *Faith that Dares to Speak* (2004) and *Freeing Celibacy* (2006).

LOUISE FULLER, History Department, National University of Ireland, Maynooth, is the author of *Irish Catholicism since 1950: The Undoing of a Culture* (2002, 2004), and co-editor with Eamon Maher and John Littleton of *Irish and Catholic? Towards an Understanding of Identity* (2006). She has contributed chapters to many volumes and published several journal articles on Irish socio-cultural history in the twentieth century with particular reference to the role and influence of the Catholic Church. Her research interests include Irish political and cultural history in the nineteenth and twentieth centuries, the history of Irish education, the interplay between religion and society and ideas and how they influence socio-cultural change. Her current research is concerned with the role of religion in the formation of identity in the Irish and broader European context.

COLUM KENNY is chairman of the Masters in Journalism Programme at Dublin City University and a member of the Broadcasting Authority of Ireland. A columnist for the *Sunday Independent*, his books include *Moments that Changed Us* (2005), a study of Ireland from 1973. His article 'Significant television: Journalism, Sex Abuse and the Catholic Church' appears in the current issue of *Irish Communications Review*.

ANDREW MADDEN was sexually abused as a child by Catholic priest Ivan Payne in Dublin in the mid 1970s. In 1995, Andrew spoke publicly for the first time about those experiences and their effects on his life. The Catholic Church in Ireland has not been the same since. Andrew is also the author of *Altar Boy: A Story of Life after Abuse* (2003).

PATRICK McCAFFERTY is a priest of the Diocese of Down and Connor. He is currently based in Dublin as a doctoral student at The Milltown Institute of Theology and Philosophy and is Parish Chaplain in Mary Immaculate, Refuge of Sinners, Rathmines.

ENDA McDONAGH is a priest of the Diocese of Tuam and Professor Emeritus of Moral Theology at St Patrick's College, Maynooth. Among his recent publications are *An Irish Reader in Moral Theology* (2009), co-edited with Vincent McNamara, and *Theology in Winter Light* (2010).

BREDA O'BRIEN is a columnist with *The Irish Times* and a second-level teacher. She is a frequent contributor to media debates on social and ethical issues. She is married to Brendan Conroy and they have four children. In the past, she has worked as a video producer, as a researcher in RTÉ and as a communications trainer.

SEAN O'CONAILL is a retired teacher of history. A contributor to Irish Catholic media since 1997, he was from 2004 to 2010 Acting Irish Coordinator for Voice of the Faithful, an international organisation founded in 2002 to support survivors of clerical sexual abuse and to work toward structural reform of the Catholic Church.

EUGENE O'BRIEN is Head of the Department of English Language and Literature in Mary Immaculate College, University of Limerick. His publications include: *Seamus Heaney – Creating Irelands of the Mind; Seamus Heaney and the Place of Writing; Seamus Heaney Searches for Answers* and *'Kicking Bishop Brennan up the Arse': Negotiating Texts and Contexts in Contemporary Irish Studies*.

GARRY O'SULLIVAN is Managing Editor of *The Irish Catholic*. He has worked for *The Irish Voice* in New York, Vatican Radio in Rome and was Communications Manager for the Jesuits. He has freelanced editorial and opinion pieces regularly for the *Irish Independent, The Examiner* and is a regular contributor to national television and radio news. He is a former student Capuchin friar.

TIMOTHY RADCLIFFE OP is a Dominican friar based in Blackfriars, Oxford. He is a former Master of the Order and is much in demand worldwide as a speaker and lecturer. His books include *Sing a New Song: The Christian Vocation* (1999), *I Call You Friends* (2001), *Seven Last Words* (2004), *What is the Point of Being Christian?* (2005) and *Why Go to Church? The Drama of the Eucharist* (2008).

SEÁN RUTH is an organisational psychologist who specialises in the areas of leadership development, conflict resolution, oppression and liberation. He is the author of two books on leadership: *Leadership and Liberation: A Psychological Approach* (2006) *and High-Quality Leadership: A Self-Assessment Guide for Individuals and Teams* (2006). His website is at www.seanruth.com.

EDDIE SHAW has forty years professional experience of understand-ing and applying the principles of risk management. He was a Director of Hibernian Group and Chairman of the National Safety Council from 2000 to 2005. He worked as a consultant Director of Communications to the Dublin Archdiocese for one year from September 2002. He is Director of Public Relations in Carr Communications. His interests are God, family, work, parish and golf – but not necessarily always in that order. His article is written in a personal capacity and he alone is re-sponsible for the views expressed.